The
Grumpy Gardener's
HANDBOOK

This book is dedicated to Leaf Lady and Old Horace, both real people, who have added to my garden enjoyment over the years in their own unique ways.

Produced by Salamander Books, 2011

First published in the United Kingdom in 2011 by
Portico Books
10 Southcombe Street
London
W14 0RA

An imprint of Anova Books Company Ltd

Illustrations by Sarah Gomes Harris

ISBN 9781907554247

A CIP catalogue record for this book is available from the British Library.

10 9 8 7 6 5 4 3 2 1

Printed and bound by Bookwell, Finland

This book can be ordered direct from the publisher at
www.anovabooks.com

The
Grumpy Gardener's
HANDBOOK

Ivor Grump

PORTICO

CONTENTS

Introduction

Some people are incredulous when you tell them that gardens are hateful places full of misery and despair. But they are. If you are one of those – how can I put it nicely – misguided simpletons who share this view, then you might want to rapidly reconsider this purchase. Indeed, if you have a generally sunny view on life, always think the best of people and see perpetual drizzle on a Sunday afternoon as a great addition to the water butt, then you probably should put this book down now. There are plenty of alternative uses for it – it's a handy enough size to stick into a chiminea. Or you could rip it up into pieces, toss it into water, squelch it up into little papier-mâché lumps and make little disposable plant pots out of it – and get your Buddhist Beginner badge at the same time.

What we deal with in all the Grumpy Handbooks, be it grumpy drivers, grumpy golfers or grumpy gardeners, is a communion of resentment and a forum of failure. Grumpy gardeners know the score when it comes to their "extra rooms outside". Gardens are enjoyed most by people who don't have to do anything in them. For the grumpy gardener who has to edge the lawn with an edging tool last sharpened in Queen Victoria's reign, it is an arena in which we are constantly obliged to tidy up. We inhabit a world where nothing ever grows up to be as good as it looked on the packet. It is a world where expensive weedkiller kills 99.9% of all known weeds…except at your particular GPS coordinates.

Even in winter when there's very little growing, things are happening in the garden that you have to do something about. There are leaves blowing in, fence panels blowing down, forgetful squirrels digging up acorns they can't remember they planted, fleece unravelling from your precious passiflora, plant pots getting frosted, cracking and spilling compost onto the patio before the wind drives it into the drains, which you can't seem to lever up any more.

Even before winter's out all the anxieties are upon you. "Where are the snowdrops? I planted 50 bulbs, surely the slugs haven't got all of them?" "Doh! Those crocuses are in the wrong place." "Why have half my daffodils gone blind?" "I thought those were red tulips I planted, these are more like orange." "Should I prune now or will a late frost penetrate further into the twigs?" "Have I pruned too much?" "Have I pruned too little?" "Where did I put the pruners anyway? On top of the shed?" "Oh…and…maybe it's a bit too late to bring that Mediterranean climate-loving bougainvillea inside."

All these thoughts run through your head when maintaining a garden. At the time of the year when Alan Titchmarsh is sitting snug and warm in a heated green oak-framed outhouse, knocking out his latest bestseller and gazing beneficently through the triple-glazed windows on a scene of dormancy and prospect, your grumpy gardener is fretting inside his house wondering when he's going to get a decent Sunday and why the fox chose to pick up one of his wellingtons and chew the end to shreds. It's not as though my wellingtons resemble a chicken carcass after all.

Your archetypal happy gardener isn't beset by doubts that he is doing the wrong thing at the wrong time. He knows when to trim and prune, when to sow and mow and he even knows how to scarify – which I like to think is what George W. Bush does to the neighbourhood children every year at Halloween.

It was ever thus for people who have to rely on the whims and vagaries of our changeable climate. Farmers are exactly the same. I know because I went to college with a whole load of them. Farmers are gloomy and pessimistic by nature. They are "glass half empty" kind of people. And it's a profession where Darwinian selection is alive and well because it's the cheery optimist hoping for the best who gets ruined financially when his wheat gets knocked down by an unexpected hailstorm. Indeed, farmers look on their crops with the same kind of attitude as I do on my garden – it's all going to go horribly wrong, you just wait and see.

You might well ask why do I bother? Why not have one of those Chelsea Flower Show gardens, which is all hard landscaping, odd sculptures, a waterfall, summer pavilion, linear box hedge and one plant in an ornate *perlato* marble planter? Or, better still, the James May garden he produced a few years back which was constructed entirely from Plasticine (they really had no idea how much he was taking the Michael).

The answer is Leaf Lady. Rider Haggard introduced us to "she who must be obeyed", a *cri de coeur* echoed by Rumpole of the Bailey. Arthur Daley had "'er indoors" in *Minder*. I have "'er outdoors", or as she has become known in recent years, Leaf Lady.

She obtained this sobriquet by her resolute determination to banish any stray leaves from our garden with the kind of zealotry seldom seen in a garden task, but more of this later. Suffice to say that under such a hardline, totalitarian regime it is hard to busk along, smelling the flowers as you go. Especially when they haven't germinated after a small unforeseen error with the propagator.

Ivor Grump.

The Old Days of Gardening

There's a bloke in our office who loves to affect a nostalgic air and say: "I can remember when all of that were fields." Which is strange considering he is about 40 and comes from Ilford. Everyone has their own perception of what the "old days" were and for my daughter, born in 1998, ancient civilisation is a time when we had VHS recorders and Wham! appeared on *Top of the Pops*.

The gardening old days for me are a time before we had the garden centre. Ah yes, in the real "old days" they were just nurseries. They would have a small car park capable of accommodating six Austin Cambridges and be based in one end of a large horticultural greenhouse. You could buy anything you wanted, providing it was something to do with roses, dahlias, twine, flowerpots or bedding plants. There was a pervading smell of greenfly spray as you walked in.

In the old days your standard gardens consisted of grass and roses, and that was about it. You had a few bedding plants for summer colour, maybe the odd shrub if you had enough space, perhaps a rockery, a small patch of vegetables or fruits bushes. Anybody who flirted with the idea of pampas grass was considered decidedly avant garde. You didn't have garden designers. You didn't have a room

11

outside. You had plants outside and you had furniture inside. Life was so much simpler then. And nobody went round calling themselves a "plantsman".

One of the vestiges of that age is the Buckingham Nursery plant catalogue. One of my few pleasures (and I do use that word very lightly) is to receive their catalogue every autumn. They are a traditional nursery specialising in a whole host of hedging plants and sundry garden items. They haven't changed the design of it much in the last 20 years and I can imagine it's been like that since the '50s. The 1350s. I suspect Geoffrey Chaucer was brought in to write the first draft of the *Nurserie Catalogue de Buckinghame* and that a parchment copy resides in the Bodleian library. You can still specify whether you want your hornbeam supplied at 1–2 feet, 2–3 feet, 3–4 feet, 4–5 feet or 5–6 feet. Marvellous.

Of course they've had to move with the times and they now have a swanky website, a garden centre and restaurant. Instead of parcelling up the bare-rooted trees into a cat's cradle of fibrous roots they have cable ties and reinforced triangular packaging. But I'd like to think that there are still 17 old men with long white beards, dressed in moleskin trousers and gaiters, sitting in a shed in Buckinghamshire wrapping up hedging plants.

Garden Gear

What was Lord Baden-Powell's motto for his new Boy Scout movement, apart from "Put down that woggle, son, it'll make you go blind"? It was "be prepared", and every grumpy gardener has to be prepared for whatever his garden has to throw at him. Just as every grumpy gardener's neighbour has to be prepared for whatever he throws at them. So it would be remiss of me not to detail the essential apparel needed to head out into that theatre of underachievement we call the garden. It's not just the plants, the weather, the wife and the lawnmower that contribute to a grumpy gardener's lot.

Chewed Wellingtons

From October to May they are an essential item in the garden, either a pair of wellingtons or some sturdy boots, or, if you're very very posh (and we are talking frightfully posh here, right up against the stopper at the end of the Posh-ometer), a pair of galoshes.

As those who bothered to read the introduction will already know, I tend to leave my wellingtons outside and a few years back the fox decided to use one of them overnight as a chew. It was annoying, but it made my wellington far more interactive with wildlife than anything else we've introduced in our garden.

While the nesting boxes we've carefully nailed to trees have been spurned by the bird population, the hedgehog hibernating spaces have been left vacant and the bait bee hives remained empty, my wellington has remained universally popular.

It wasn't the first time it's hosted wildlife and I'm sure it won't be the last. I've become fairly used to having spiders vacate the space in a hurry as they've sensed the arrival of a size 8–11 sock, my foot included. The worst thing I've ever found in the bottom was a dead mouse. Thankfully it had been dead for some time and got to the dry, dessicated stage – so much so that I thought I'd put my foot on a clump of dead leaves that had got in there. When I pulled the leaves out they were grey and had a tail. My wife thought this was extraordinarily funny, not because I'd stood on it, but the fact that it had probably died from the smell in there.

Apart from functioning as a wildlife play area, they can also act as small water butts and collect rainfall for you if you're stupid enough to leave them standing upright outside. Which of course I am. At least, the right one can become a rain butt. The left one has a hole in the instep created by a 6" nail from the time I was tearing down the old shed and wasn't particularly careful where I was walking. That's a dance I don't want to do again in a hurry.

Between May and September I forget they have a leak and only become reacquainted with the fact when water comes oozing through in October when I start to dig over the beds.

Gloves

Gloves are an important but not an essential part of the grumpy gardener's armour in his ongoing fight to maintain order in the garden. I like to think I don't need them for anything except handling thorny stems. I'm a man, I've harvested potatoes on a commercial basis in my time, I can handle it.

In the autumn I will eschew the glove and rush to embrace a pile of fallen sugar maple leaves only to gather up a bundle of yellow and gold that smells suspiciously of cat poo. And then I realise it's not a worm cast that I picked up as well…

But do I learn my lesson? Five minutes later and I'm thrusting my still ungloved hand into gutters to clear out leaves only to find, to my great amusement, that it's not just deciduous leaves that have collected. There's holly in there too! (I'd like to find out some natural predators for holly and give them a really good home.)

Even when you do don some gloves you're not safe. A lot of garden gloves advertise themselves as thornproof, which is one of the greatest lies of the 21st century.

We understand the concept of a bulletproof vest as a protective garment that will stop bullets getting through. A thornproof glove hardly stops anything; it's the wimpiest of the wimpy. It impedes tiny rose-like thorns very slightly, so that you don't get the whole spur dug into your hand. All they're designed to cater for is thorn appeasement. When it comes to big woody thorns it runs up the white flag straight away. As for long woody spines on hedging stock like hawthorn, quickthorn or whitethorn, well, you might as well be wearing nothing at all.

What you really need is a pair of big gauntlets made out of the same kind of material they use to make wicket-keepers gloves. Then you could truly say they were thorn proof and go into bat.

Old This and Old That

In winter, the plan is to wear an old jacket or old, scraggy fleece for gardening. In spring it's probably going to be a seen-better-days jumper and shirt that's required. In summer the best thing would be an old shirt or T-shirt. And all these can be teamed with a derelict pair of jeans whose knees have worn through.

When clothes get a bit careworn and should really be thrown out, they get saved by the reprieve, "I can still use them for gardening." But when it actually comes round to gardening... I ignore them completely and don't bother getting changed.

The only time I'll make a concession and make the effort to put on old shambolic gardening clothes is when I know I have to do some heavy digging. Sod's law (quite literally) in these circumstances will dictate that before I can get started I'll need to take a trip up to the garden centre, for which I can't be bothered to get changed either.

In these circumstances, un-suited and badly wellington booted, I feel like Jessie from *The Fast Show* as I walk in through the automatic door. "Today I have mostly been diggin' moi turnips." In fact, I really should get an old jacket, rip the buttons off and tie it up with baler twine to complete the effect. Ironically, when I'm dressed like this at the garden centre, people will often ask me for plant advice. It's happily given and always gratefully received.

Old Hat

For me, a hat is an essential item of garden wear. It stops me getting sunburnt in summer and totally sopping wet in winter. There are two essential elements to garden headgear apart from the really obvious ones, which are a) That it fits and b) That it doesn't make you look like a Breton fisherman. The first prerequisite is that it's washable, because sooner or later you're going to put a muddy hand or glove on it. Or it's going to fall into the pond.

The second is that it doesn't have bright colours, which attract insects that might want to come and pollinate you. I used to have a Formula 1 Red Bull team cap, all vibrant reds and yellows, which was a big hit with bumble bees whose eyesight isn't the best.

Indeed one of the top practical jokes you can play on a gardener is to get hold of some moth pheromone and spray it on his hat. Many species of day-flying moths have an extraordinary scenting ability and will fly for miles to get to a female. When I was at college one of the horticulture students managed to get hold of some of this pheromone and sprayed it onto a lecturer's cricket jumper during the staff versus students cricket match. The moment he came to the crease, moths started appearing from everywhere. After five minutes he was definitely feeling the moth love and looked like a small roost for the creatures. Sadly you don't see the substance advertised so much on eBay, but if you know a student who can get hold of the stuff…

Naked Gardening

You may have seen them on television already, but there's an older, slightly hippyish couple with a grand garden somewhere in Wiltshire who pop up on gardening programmes from time to time. They don't need to make too many choices of what to wear in the garden as their big thing is gardening in the buff.

This sounds hazardous in the extreme and would make me even grumpier, should I be forced to do it. (Though it would give Mrs MacDonald next door something to focus on with her binoculars). For a start there's all that sun cream to smother yourself with. Then there are the little midgy biting insects that live in grassland – it would be the equivalent of handing them an open buffet in the shape of your legs and ankles. You'd get lacerated by leaves, prickled by thorns, poked by twigs and you wouldn't dare bend over in case you backed into a red hot poker. That's not to mention burrowing insects such as masonry bees who are constantly on the lookout for dark comfy crevices in which to make their home. It doesn't bear thinking about.

What Your Wellingtons Say About You

Never judge a book by its cover but always judge a gardener by her or his wellies. If you own a pair of wellington boots like the ones listed below, there is a slim chance that you're the exception to the rule. But probably not. The scientific rigour used in devising this guide to wellies is as robust as any you're going to get in this book.

Blue and shiny.
You never go gardening but you want people to think you do.

Pink and spotty.
You're a girly girl at heart and your garden will be filled with bright pinks and whites and purples. Either that or you're three years old and have just started at your first playgroup.

Floral (and you're a girl).
You worry about how you look while you're gardening. You're probably built like a female tag wrestler or work on the Russian whaling fleet and want to add an element of femininity to your massive hulk.

19

Floral (and you're a bloke).
You have small sensitive feet and simply adore pansies.

Fashion designer wellies.
You never go gardening, you use your wellies for walking round National Trust properties or on the train to work if there's snow.

Black (or green) and battered.
You're a real gem, a true hardy gardening perennial. Those gardeners who have additional customization inflicted by vermin are true gents.

Fur-lined – or trimmed with fur.
They probably weren't destined to cosset your foot while gardening, they were more likely intended to keep your feet warm on the touchline as you follow the progress of your son/grandson on the sporting field of play while roundly berating the ref-er-ee!

Green with a fancy heel and leather straps.
What are you doing in the garden? You should be out point-to-pointing or three-day-eventing.

Union Jack wellies.
You're a tourist.

Black with leather effect and metal studs.
You should be at Glastonbury.

Red wellies.
You're Paddington bear.

Neighbours

They may never come into your garden, but your neighbours can have a big effect on what you do in the garden and how pleasant it is to spend time out there. When you move to a new house, the seller never tips you off that the people either side are complete fruitcakes. Like Forrest Gump said, life is like a box of chocolates, you never know what you're going to get. Although, like a box of chocolates, you often end up with a nut you don't want. I'm perhaps lucky in that two out of three of my neighbours are nutters. I don't have the full set of chocolates that are left by Boxing Day morning.

Mrs MacDonald Wears the Troosers

Now I'm not saying that our next door neighbour to the right is a mean, nosey, twisted, interfering dried-up old stick – I think that's just what I wrote on her Christmas card. Only joking, we actually wrote "Happy Christmas, Mrs MacDonald" on the card, which featured the worst piece of children's artwork we could find: three kings on three four-legged beasts – which could have been camels but equally could have been pigs – bearing gifts, plus a jet in the top corner. It took me ages to draw.

In some ways she's worse, in some way she's better. Pleasant to your face, but the moment your back is turned she'll bitch like a footballer's wife to the neighbours... though I can't imagine many Premier League WAGs bitching on the subject of my fence.

Ever since her husband was called by the good lord she's had too much time on her hands. "Don [pronounced D-o-o-o-h-h-n] was an executive director and drove a top-of-the-range Mercedes saloon," she's keen to tell you, so she's not short of a bob or two.

She employs a gardener for two hours a week; a beleaguered-looking man in his mid-40s otherwise known as "the laddie". It's part gardening, part role-play. She sees herself in the role of a more heterosexual Vita Sackville-West, standing in her tweed skirt with hands on hips, directing the grand planting schemes – two foxgloves here, a begonia there. He sees himself in the role of cutting the grass and getting the hell out of there before she starts picking holes in what he's done and how clean he's left the lawnmower.

Fence Wars

The only real bone of contention between me and Mrs MacDonald is the rickety fence between our two properties that she insists is my responsibility. As she's been there for 30-odd years I can hardly dispute that it's not. Whenever we get talking about any particular subject – children, neighbourhood watch, television, Afghanistan – she manages to steer the conversation back towards the fence, and when it's going to be replaced. It's not hard because we're normally talking over it. She always gives me the impression that once there are new fence panels between us she's going to win a gardening prize – Best Small Garden of Britain – and that I'm the only thing holding her back.

The previous occupant of our house, also an elderly Scot, was promising to replace it up until the time he died aged 92. Mrs MacDonald clearly thinks that in some respects Old George shuffled off this mortal coil in order to get out of replacing the fence.

She still brings up the time that she and Don went to Madeira for a fortnight and came back to find that George had – cue dramatic music – entered her garden without prior permission and inserted reinforcing bars "on our side of the property" in an effort to prop it up cheaply. It must have been like the Cuban missile crisis.

Crafty old George obviously realised that the only way to extend the life of the fence was to get into her garden and that she'd never let him do that. I have to say, for a fence constructed in the early 1930s, it's not doing badly. When the Grump dial is switched particularly high I'll start to tell her that I've approached the council to have it listed as a historic linear structure. I suggest that students of garden design history may want to come and view it in the context of suburban development in the 1930s, or perhaps using the pretext that the Battle of Britain was "probably" fought in the skies over this fence.

Achtung, Schnell, Schnell!

I have to confess, it does lean impressively in the wind and whenever gravity gets the better of one or two sections, Mrs MacDonald is sure to let me know. She surveils it with binoculars, very much like the Stasi used to keep an eye on their Berlin-based boundary. Should there be any degree of lean beyond 5 degrees, she pops kindly informative notes through our letter box. Which is not quite how the Stasi used to go about things, but she's just as efficient.

I'm then obliged to trudge out there and wedge it back up again. Some sections are so weak they have had to be wired to trees now. There will come a time when I have the money to replace it, but I like to think that leaving it gives her a reason for living. She's so determined to outlast it that installing a new one would be the end of her.

Legend of the Weasel

My neighbour in the garden behind is not as engaging as Mrs MacDonald. For legal reasons I can't give his real name, but his real nickname is "The Weasel". Anyone who grew up with *Wind in the Willows* will know that it's not an affectionate nickname. It's a nickname based on two things – one, he looks like a weasel; two, he acts like a weasel.

We rarely see him in the garden, not because he's nocturnal and rarely comes out of his burrow till sunset. It's because, thankfully, there's a six-foot fence between us. When we do catch glimpses of him, true to form, he's darting and furtive. He gained the "Weasel" moniker one January after southern England had endured a prolonged period of rain, when the last place you'd want to spend any time was the garden. One Sunday afternoon an agitated Mrs MacDonald appeared at the front door to tell us there was now a stream in our garden and that it was pouring water into hers – which is slightly downhill from us. Her garden was getting badly waterlogged, not only that, the rapidly gathering pond looked like it was going to rise up and flood in through her patio doors.

So it was on with the wellingtons and out into the garden to investigate. Mrs M was keen to lay the blame squarely on Old George and the concrete paths he'd created in the 1960s, which collected and channelled water out of our garden – "it's not your fault, luvvie, it's that old devil, he didn't give two hoots" she said. Sure enough, you didn't have to be a water diviner to work out that it was flowing at an impressive rate down one of the lateral concrete paths. But it was only doing that because it was flooding out of the Weasel's garden at a similar rate of knots.

A quick look over the fence revealed that the Weasel had created a system of drainage channels that collected water and directed it out of his garden, under the fence and into mine. From whence it flowed down the concrete path and into Mrs MacDonald's, threatening to inundate her. I may have been simply the conduit but I was livid.

I stomped round to his house and demanded to know why he'd created a system that was deliberately anti-social – "the water has to go somewhere" was his weaselly reply. "My lawn's being crucified. Anyway, we live on a hill, where do you think it's going to go...?"

I have to confess, the temptation to punch him was very great, and though I was fighting the cause of a frightened septuagenarian who was about to be flooded out by this spineless, chinless little git I knew it wouldn't look good in court to have lamped someone at least six inches shorter than me. Who was a member of the ferret family.

'Here, Foxy Foxy!'

The great thing about falling out with neighbours is you're not limited to the ones you share boundaries with. You can easily develop a loathing for people a couple of gardens away (as we'll find out with bonfires, below). This is particularly the case when they insist on feeding the local fox population.

While you're doing your best to eradicate them from your garden by painstakingly filling up all the holes they dig under the fence, some arse is encouraging them to breed by feeding them chicken bones. The minute that supply runs out and they've developed a taste for Chicken Tikka Masala, they're all over your bins trying to get their teeth into leftover Rogan Josh and Lamb Dupiaza.

There must be a den with cubs a few gardens up from us because you can hear them yapping and yowling all summer long. These fox-loving idiots act like these animals are some rare species of white rhino and probably bask in the self-satisfied glow that they're a big friend of nature.

Bonfire of the Pleasantries

Lighting a bonfire is one of those activities you're never quite sure is within the byelaws or not. There's a widely perceived wisdom that they are legal providing you have them after 6 o'clock in the evening. The truth of the matter is that you can have them whenever you want, any time of the day or night, providing you make them smelly enough.

In the real, practical world you have to be thick-skinned (to an estate agent level) or very stupid to go and light a bonfire during the day, while your neighbours might have washing on the line or be out enjoying themselves in the garden. But it happens. And it's not just your next door neighbour it affects, it spreads resentment over several gardens downwind. Remember the old Bisto adverts with the curling aromatic wisp tantalising people's nostrils? Like that but in reverse.

The most outrageous case of bonfire in *flagrante* was when somebody a few doors up from us lit a bonfire one glorious sunny Sunday afternoon in June. Within minutes there was a deputation of about four neighbours on his doorstep demanding that he put it out – or we would put it out for him. When he saw the angry faces gathered there, the penny dropped. He obviously hadn't given it a second thought. And I don't think he's had one since.

That's not to say I don't like the smell of a bonfire. When the days are short in winter it can be very atmospheric to pick up the scent of a bonfire on the breeze. It helps give the sense of passing seasons – freshly pruned apple tree twigs crackle and burn on some distant fire. But not from my trees if it's January.

Overhanging Branches

Things your neighbours grow close to their boundary can be very irritating. One thing I have to say about the Weasel is that even though he may channel half a reservoir through my garden from time to time, he grows nice low shrubs and trims them impeccably…with his snouty, weasely little paws.

One of my previous neighbours decided it would be a great idea to grow some bamboo in the corner of his garden. Bamboo can be very invasive and soon we were all growing bamboo in the corners of our gardens – me, the couple behind and the couple diagonally opposite him. How grateful were we for those free plants…?

A couple of years later I retaliated with some ground elder. I didn't plant it deliberately, I saw it there one day by the edge of his fence and turned and looked the other way. Anyone who's been plagued with it will know that ground elder is a complete nuisance. However I have managed to find an ecological control, something that will predate it and keep it back to manageable levels. She's called Leaf Lady.

As part of your neighbourly rights you are allowed to

chop anything off that ventures over your side of the fence, so interfering branches can be lopped off at will. You also have a duty to deposit it back over your neighbour's fence in case he wants it for something or other, you know, like the famous stick sculptures he's always making, or for his charcoal furnace.

In practice, I'm a vigorous lopper of Mrs MacDonald's lively yew tree, but I've never bothered to toss it back for the laddie to deal with as it seems unnecessarily provocative. The same for her very delicious apples that overhang our garden, which are harvested between 11 and 12.30 on a Sunday morning when she goes off to church and the observation tower is empty.

Back to the Roots

Another cross you have to bear for having neurotic neighbours is when they start to think that trees you planted are plotting to undermine their foundations. We used to live next to someone who was nicknamed "The Witch". (Like I said before, we always get nutters.) She didn't have a black cat, but she did have a few warts and her hair was jet black, provided she remembered to dye it every month. Her eyes were like coal, too. She had it in for my Indian bean tree. I love Indian bean trees, but she got it fixed in her head that it was too close to her rear extension. This is an extension her ex-husband had casually tacked onto the side of the house with no great reference to the planning system, before legging it to France with another woman.

The Indian bean tree was actually closer to our house than hers but she would harass my wife about it endlessly, so in the end it was easier just to chop the thing down. It had only got to about four metres high, but she'd been reading how high they could grow. And she obviously couldn't find a spell in her book that covered the situation. Part of the reason I acquiesced so easily was that I felt slightly guilty about a nasty incident with my bees. I had a couple of hives in a quiet corner of the garden and one Saturday in the summer I'd done a routine inspection, going through the frames, which stirs the workers up and makes them a bit agitated.

Our neighbour came into the garden and a couple of the bees that were circulating, waiting for the hubbub to go down, got stuck in her over-lacquered hair. Now bees have hooky feet that latch onto things and even though they would have wanted to get away from the high concentration of dye and hairspray they couldn't. And their natural reaction when they're frightened is to sting.

I came back into the garden to hear a wailing noise, a dreadful moan somewhere between a poor ghost impersonation and a bad pornographic movie as she rushed back into the house beating at the two hapless bees that had got stuck in her barnet and stung her on the head.

I got my good karma back by chopping the Indian bean tree down.

Do it the Grumpy Gardener Way

Faced with the same situation of a large, mature tree threatening your property, experts believe you should try conciliation before taking any kind of action. However, an expert grumpy gardener's advice is to hop over the fence while your neighbours are out and hammer some discreet copper nails into the trunk close to the ground. Certainly not at the level where they would be discovered by a chainsaw chopping it down after it has suffered death by copper poisoning.

Barbecues

Everyone loves a barbecue on a sunny day. Well, maybe not vegetarians so much, but they've only got themselves to blame. Even so, it gets a bit tiresome when your neighbours have a barbecue on what seems like every sunny day of the summer. Which immediately prompts the question from your children, "Can WE have a barbecue...?" To which the answer is, "No, we've had one this summer already and it took me about a week and a half to scrub the grill clean."

Now that's what someone should have presented on *Dragons' Den* five years ago. The minute some sweating, trembling entrepreneur steps into the spotlight and reveals the first self-cleaning barbecue grill they would have a million sales.

Living next to prolific barbecue-ers is torture. Especially when they're posh and can afford fish. The smell of grilled fish instantly transports the wife and I back to the Greek tavernas of our courting days, when there were only two types of fish in the Aegean – swordfish and sardines, a time when we didn't have a mortgage, we didn't have children and everything was a lot firmer.

When the scent of fish drifts over from next door, the temptation to go round and swipe some from on top of their top-of-the-range Outback grill is sometimes overwhelming.

As is the temptation to switch on the lawn sprinkler with the hose pressure set to maximum! "Oops, sorry, did it really carry that far...?" .

Jobs to Avoid in January

Look in some of the helpful garden journals and they'll have an agenda of little garden jobs to keep you busy throughout the year. It's almost like they assume you'll enjoy being out there and need the slimmest of pretexts to tear yourself away from Sky Sports.

Creosoting the fence.
Logic tells you that this is the best time of the year to do it. The perennials have died back, there's little or no growth going on in the beds so you're going to do the least amount of damage to your plants. But hey, there's going to be more daylight and the weather will have picked up in February – do it then.

Clearing out the shed.
Why risk taking all your nice dry, carefully stacked equipment out of the shed only to see it get wet in a sudden shower. And you've been through all that stuff before, that broken petrol mower that last ran in 1987 could still come in useful.

Pruning the fruit trees.
This could be a bit risky if we have a sudden cold snap and the frost penetrates deep into the twigs and branches that you've just cut. This is definitely a February job.

Rake out the moss in the lawn.
Not sure if this is a good idea either with the lawn still so wet.

Take the lawnmower for a service.
And have you seen how much the local mower shop is charging? It's daylight robbery. It's a Honda mower not a Honda Civic! If they're going to charge that much for

sharpening a blade and changing the oil and spark plug then you're going to do it yourself. But not this month, obviously.

Plant some early veg under cloches.
Doh! Putting out cloches to warm the soil is like giving all the bugs in your garden a centrally heated rest home and filling it with food to munch their way through winter. You want to leave those beds barren and cold and chill the little blighters into submission, you don't want them cosseted.

Replace any broken or wobbly fence panels.
You'd like to, but with your new green eco-credentials you're not sure that it's the best move for the planet. It's far more environmentally friendly to make do and mend.

January is the perfect month for checking through your seed packets. Find a box and file them in the date they should be sown.
Yeah, like that's going to happen.

Herbaceous perennials can be lifted and divided in January.
Then what do you do? You haven't got enough space in the garden as it is. Maybe the plant sales stand at the school fair would benefit from it – or maybe they won't after that narky letter they sent home about your son's unfortunate gender stereotyping in his artwork, namely his piece, "Mummy running over animals and having an accident, again".

Check out your gardening tools.

Take a good look at your gardening equipment in this fallow period before the onset of spring. Could it be cleaner, sharper, better oiled? Yes. Are you going to do it? No.

Tidy the pond in readiness for the frogs and toads that will soon be arriving.

I'm not tidying the *****y pond. How do you "tidy" a pond anyway – take out the supermarket trolley and get the fish to swim in geometrically pleasing patterns?

Keep the bird table well-stocked.

They've got nothing to complain about. They have enough fat balls to get them through till March. And if they want a rich variety of seeds, insects, nuts, peanuts, sunflower hearts and suet berry treats they can go three doors up. I'm not feeding the squirrels. Unless it's to the fox. Feeding the birds may be a kindly activity, but it starts an almighty turf war. The blue tits take it in turns to scare each other off the feeder, then the robins join in. Then the jays come in and try and prey on the blue tits. Half an hour after you put the fat balls out it's WWIII in the garden. And that's before the squirrels join in.

Review garden notes about successes and failures in the garden and greenhouse.

The successes aren't going to take long. Unless "failed to kill" can be listed as a success…

The Garden Centre

When it comes to modern garden centres I get a bit schizophrenic. The bit of me responsible for getting my wallet out hates them. The bit of me that responds to bright shiny things struggles to resist. They are seductive little madames, servants of Mammon. You have to keep your eyes averted from the shelves as you walk in or you're in big trouble. I go in there intent on buying a 70-litre bag of multi-compost – nothing else – and half an hour later I'm walking out with a multi-nozzle Hozelock spray head, a dazzling new variety of hydrangea, an interesting variation on vermiculite and a combined garden clock-digital maximum/minimum thermometer. On the way home I suddenly realise I forgot to buy the multi-compost. You have to be strong in a garden centre.

It never used to be like this…

Old Horace's

We used to have Old Horace. Old Horace's garden centre was at the edge of town and fitted the image of the traditional nursery outlined in the introduction, selling a narrow range of garden essentials. If you wanted a spade, you had a choice of two. If you wanted something fancy, like an extendable tree pruner, you had to order it. It was based in an old horticultural greenhouse with a cash desk that looked more like the counter in the *Two Ronnies'* classic hardware store routine – "four candles?" Behind it was a small office with the door permanently jammed open in which someone had placed an old desk, a Fax machine designed by Thomas Edison, and a chair in desperate need of upholstery. The two lever-arch files had long been over-run, the whole room was awash with about seven years' worth of catalogues, invoices and paperwork. Doing Old Horace's accounts must have been like an Indiana Jones adventure.

Old Horace himself was not unlike Ronnie Barker's character, Arkwright, in *Open All Hours.* He was spectacularly mean. To get into the garden centre building there was a sliding door, and there was another to allow you into the plant sales area beyond. Both had very large, Please Shut the Door signs on either side. Woe betide you if you left either sliding door open in winter when precious heat would escape. Forget the old American sales mantra that the customer was always right, at Old Horace's the customer was a flaming nuisance. He would usually allow you to leave it open once without saying anything, after that you were fair game. Sometimes it would be a piercing whistle to remind you, sometimes a not very jokey, "Were you born in a barn?" If it was an older customer he'd assume they wouldn't be able to hear him properly: "The door! Shut the door! No, the door. No, it slides. Yes. Ye-e-e-e-e-s."

One of his regular customers bought him a football referee's whistle for Christmas, which he thought was a real hoot. He jokingly asked why he hadn't been given a notebook to take their names down as well.

You would never get a smiley, "Have a nice afternoon" from Old Horace, but his hardcore clientele loved him.

That Plant's Almost Dead

One of Old Horace's endearing traits was never to give any money off anything for any reason. As far as he was concerned the 1979 Sale of Goods Act was witchcraft. I once had a protracted argument with him over some Yorkstone-look paving slabs, which after one shower of rain looked very much like ordinary paving slabs again. Horace was having none of it, that's the way they were, he could have told me that when I bought them if I'd bothered to ask... I would have got further if I'd addressed my complaint to the paving slab.

He was a canny supplier of bulk materials, too. In the days before the large bulk bags he had the ability to judge a ton of sand to the nearest three grains, you never got a couple of wheelbarrows extra just to be on the safe side.

The thing that drew most of his regulars back was that he would always have a really interesting range of plants. He would stock shrubs and trees that garden centres double his size didn't have, so it was always a pleasure to go there and browse. You could spend a happy half hour drifting along the A-Z of shrubs, dally a while in the alpines, saunter around the herbs. It was never ever busy.

Occasionally, you'd spot a choice shrub that had suffered some kind of die-back, or some yellowing, or that was basically sound but had some lopsided growth and approach Horace with a view to having the price reduced. Not a chance. Every time you thought you had a water-tight case for getting money off he'd have the perfect riposte. "That's got a vigorous root, it'll grow back in no time." Or, "stick some Miracle Grow on that and it'll disappear in a couple of weeks," and he'd stride off down to the fertiliser shelves and bring you back an extra product to sell you along with the ailing plant.

Suffer the Little Children

Considering he was so brilliant at persuading you to buy things when he put his mind to it, the chances of him ever introducing a "Giftware" department were slim to none. Horace's only concession to the impulse purchase was an ice cream freezer by the cash desk. Everything else that was arranged for the last second purchase was handy rather than gifty.

At Christmas he sold the usual fare of tree decorations and yuletide sundries, but there was never going to be a wider gift range or a Santa's Grotto. I once suggested to him – yes, to his face – that he would make a fantastic Santa, to which I got a very satisfying, "not b****y likely". Horace hated children.

There were signs up all round, both inside and outside, that children had to be accompanied by adults at all times.

He hated the casual damage they could do by running round unsupervised and tipping over his pots, or playing hide and seek in the shrubs and breaking off branches.

Instead of creating things they might be interested in, his view was to ban them and he really didn't care if their parents were offended when he told them off (that's the children, not the parents). If he'd had the time I'm sure he would have created a little play area for them, the equivalent of the Poison Garden at Alnwick, but without the warning signs. He was a true grumpy garden centre owner.

The Demise of Old Horace

It was like hearing the news that a close friend had gone. I swung by Old Horace's one day on the hunt for some ant powder, only to find him unnaturally quiet; close to tears in fact. It didn't take long to find out why. The lease on his garden centre site had come up for renewal and the landlord was going to double it. There was no way he could sustain the business on that kind of rent. As it was, he puttered along in business, selling a few shrubs and trays of bedding plants here, providing a little bit of garden maintenance there, but it wasn't a huge turnover. At peak times he'd have 20 cars there and two people serving, but on most weekdays there'd be five or six cars and one girl on the till. This dramatic hike in the rent was most definitely the end.

In due course Horace closed his gates and the site went dark for about a year and a half before a big garden centre chain took over the site and bulldozed all traces of the plant terraces and the old greenhouses. In their place they erected a palatial edifice, with a swish restaurant, garden furniture sales and automatic doors that didn't need a notice reminding you to close them behind you.

It was soulless and staffed by people who knew more about barcodes than plants. I wanted to boycott it, but it was just too damned convenient. But whenever I'm there, wandering around the wide, child-friendly rows, I never fail to look around me and work out where I would be standing in Horace's old garden centre. Would this be the hardy perennials or the fruit trees? I also wonder if he's been back and what he thinks of this new palace of gardening delights. Especially Santa's Grotto at Christmas.

I-Spy at the Garden Centre

In my last grumpy outing, *The Grumpy Golfer's Handbook*, I postulated that if you go up to a golf driving range there will always be at least one Japanese golfer belting a bucket of balls into the wide blue yonder. Similarly, whenever you go to a garden centre there will always be at least one middle-aged lady in a quilted body warmer, or gilet, browsing the shelves and the plant racks.

For all I know it may be the standard issue of garden centre store detectives, but it is now your duty to play the quilted body warmer game whenever you venture in (barring the off-season, July–August).

Furniture Envy

Something you didn't get when you went up to Old Horace's was furniture envy. Unless you were envious of an old slatted metal folding chair that looked as though it had been nicked from a lawn tennis club in the 1930s. Walk into a modern garden centre and you are assailed by the sight of fabulous patio furniture that wouldn't look out of place on the terrace of some exclusive French Riviera hotel (with a uniformed waiter ready to take your order for a 25 euro cappuccino). Beautifully sculpted wicker banquettes are lined up next to low, teak-framed sofas with deep, luxurious cream-coloured cushions. Overhead hang elegantly engineered, pendulous, tan-coloured awnings, like the sails of some lateen-rigged Arab dhow. The tables are laid out for that perfect Mediterranean déjeuner à quatre and you can imagine sauntering out there to sit with friends on the hottest day in summer, a glass of chilled prosecco in hand.

Then you look at the price… and then envy sets in.

So now you imagine it on a miserable summer's day, where unforecast rain has set in and is dripping off the end of the canvas onto easily soiled cushions – "why did we get that colour anyway?" – while all the time you turn over in your mind where you're going to store the whole unwieldy edifice over winter. That's better.

I Blame Chris Packham

Do you know what a little owl looks like? A proper little owl, not a big owl a long way away. Well, if you didn't and always yearned for an owl in your garden then a trip to the modern garden centre might soon avail you of that pleasure. Because now essential gardening accessories are being squeezed out in favour of peripheral things like wildlife boxes. No need to install a whole barn in your efforts to attract a barn owl into your garden when a simple box can bag you a barn owl or a little owl.

Designed by wildlife experts, the Little Owl Box is the perfect space for an aspiring little owl to set up family. It's not just the result of some clumsy woodworker who was trying to build a blue tit box and got his dimensions wrong – even though to look at it you'd think that.

Why anyone would want what is basically a farmland animal in their garden, hooting to keep them awake at nights and rarely making an appearance in daylight hours, is hard to understand. Little owls are not endangered and they are not even a native species, they were introduced to this country in the late Victorian era. It's like putting the flying equivalent of a grey squirrel box in your garden.

How About a Bat Box?

Now you're talking. I wouldn't mind a bat box because I know bats are around and they're perfectly adapted for a suburban environment. And they don't have a tendency to go "tuuuu-wiiiit" or "wooooooooo" when you're trying to get some sleep on a warm summer's night.

And I suppose I've still got a bit of residual bat guilt after we found a dead one enmeshed in the spokes of one of the children's bikes that was left strapped to the top of the car one night. The bat's famous sonar obviously didn't pick up that spokes were a severe obstacle to flight and also – quite understandably – hadn't expected to encounter a child's bike six foot up in the air in a place that was normally a free-fly zone.

There are a variety of nice bat boxes you can buy at garden centres, as well as the conventional blue tit box and robin box.

And There's More

But it doesn't stop there. You can now buy a whole range of bespoke lodgings for wildlife visitors. How about a sturdy hedgehog habitat made of some satisfyingly chunky wood? Or alternatively, opt for the variety that has a roof of synthetic leaves that looks like a cross between an old OO-gauge railway modeller's tunnel and the Wombles' attempt to restyle the Greenwich Dome.

If you're not sure that hedgehogs can get into your garden, what about something for our amphibian friends? You can now buy an off-the-shelf frog/toad house made from wood to help Beatrix Potter's friends spend a comfortable winter. Presumably, if this proved popular you could either extend to create a frog/toad villa complex or a small frog/toad housing estate. There's also the more bijou Frogitat, which is a ceramic home from home.

I wanted to ask the sales assistant whether this was also suitable for toads or if you had to buy a separate Toaditat, but my wife said they would spot that I was being facetious. I was quite serious about the Newtitat, though.

That's all very well for the more telegenic creatures but what about looking after the creepy crawlies, the bugs that sustain the ecosystem? They're catered for, too. You can shell out on a butterfly haven, or a nesting box for solitary bees, a home for lacewings, or, if you've got a load of cash, the equivalent of a big bug hotel with over-wintering canes and a myriad of carefully separated nooks and crannies to cater for all kinds of different insects who don't necessarily want to meet up and eat each other. And if you have money beyond sense, you can cough up for a solar-powered insect theatre.

'Lights, Camera, Action!'

And there's even more! Such is our great love of nature programmes that you can now buy a specialised nesting box with its own camera and cabling pre-installed. Who needs the BBC and *Springwatch* (which for some reason starts in summer) when you can spend unlimited hours watching your own nesting birds.

Maybe I'd buy one too if I didn't already know that I'd be staring at a wooden floor for 365 days of the year. Every bird box I have ever made or bought has been shunned by the bird public. Nary a viewing. Not a single twig deposited inside.

I built an over-wintering box for hedgehogs once and filled it with straw – they didn't want to know.

I have a fine cedar WBC hive (the old traditional type with pagoda-style roof lifts) ready and waiting for a stray swarm of bees. We had a swarm over the road and they preferred the hedge.

Even if by some freak of nature a bird did decide to nest in my camera box I'm sure a spider would build a web over the lens and sit in the centre, creating *Frightwatch*, from which my daughter would never recover.

Bird Feeders

Old Horace didn't really believe in stock rotation. His major concession to retail presentation was occasionally wiping the dust off boxes. These days in garden centres they will have stock plan-o-grams. Come a certain day and all the garden furniture goes out and the Christmas stock comes in. Then in spring all the thermal socks go out and all the seed racks come in. For Mother's Day there's a big push on house plants and a few pocket money presents. Bulbs will go large in autumn, then dwindle as the snowdrops break cover. Then the dazzling array of barbecues elbow their way back in. One day you can be looking down the shelves for a hose attachment and the next week you go back and there's a wall of bird feed staring at you. Familiar stuff moves around, carried like flotsam on the tide of seasonal presentation.

Nestling up against the wildlife boxes there is a

phenomenal array of bird feeders. So many, in fact, that I decided to count them. Our local garden centre sells 63 different types of bird feeder in 88 different locations, i.e. they have so many of the favourite ones that they'll double stack them on displays or double face them on shelves.

God in heaven why do we need 63 types of bird feeder?!

When it comes to equipment for the more garden-oriented chores, such as pricking out – something that every seed grower will have to do – they have one variety of dibber, one variety of widger and that's your blinking lot.

The logic of this is plain to see when you take a look across the aisle from the bird feeders. There sits a mountain of bird feed, each neatly designed to fit into the designated feeder. They want you to keep coming back and filling up. It's a cunning plan to get you to part with your cash.

Bird Feed Junkies

In some respects, buying a bird feeder is like going on heroin. Once you get hooked, you can't give it up. You're compelled to keep going because you've got a wild bird dependency – they're relying on you to provide the fat balls or the sunflower seeds with real dried insects. You have to keep going till spring.

For someone who buys a job lot of fat balls from his local hardware store and slings them in a careworn dispenser every December (in a location the squirrel hasn't figured out how to get to) I was staggered at what you could buy.

There's robin seed insect blend, blue tit seed insect blend, high-energy de luxe seed blend (presumably for discerning wild birds who are running marathons). There's finch blend, hedgerow blend, woodland blend and songbird blend (presumably with some kind of throat lozenge that aids their singing ability).

You can have sunflower seeds, nyjer seeds, peanuts and mealworm. Should your garden birds prefer a fat-rich diet you can buy them a berry suet feed, a fruit suet feed, a coco fat feed, a seed-and-insect suet feed, a peanut suet feed. There's even a company that markets fruit suet "treats", which is a bizarre concept for wild animals who might find it hard to recognise that they are some kind of special teatime indulgence.

Dogs perform an act of intelligence – they get a treat. Wild birds…well, they just turn up and it's there waiting for them. They probably don't all congregate on the back fence afterwards, bloated like avian Mr Pickwicks and turn to each other and go "…reckon that must have been her birthday."

Ultimately the Parakeets

The marketing for these seeds is very clever, almost aspirational. Everybody wants lovely songbirds in their gardens. We've all seen *Mary Poppins.* But are you going to get them by buying songbird mix? What's the word-of-beak going to be like in the roosts and worm-tugging gardens of suburbia – will the right birds get to hear about what you're offering? And wouldn't it be much simpler to annihilate all the bird-preying local cats instead.

It made me think that having specific bird mixes could go a lot further than just finches, robins and blue tits. Why stop there? What I particularly like to see in the garden are wrens

– yet they don't get a mention. There should be a wren mix, a thrush mix, an owl mix, a bat mix, a little warbler mix and, not forgetting, a prawn-flavoured osprey mix for luring all those fish-loving ospreys into your garden.

While I was making notes for this book, a lady came past the aisle on a Motability scooter. She saw me with my notepad and asked me what I was doing. I told her I was researching for a section of a book and that I was flabbergasted at the sheer variety of seeds you could buy for garden birds. "It doesn't matter what you buy, dear," she confided, "the parakeets get it all." And it's true, where we live we're within reach of one of the many south-east parakeet roosts and they are like the smash and grab merchants of the bird world. They arrive in a mob, do a feeder over, and they're noisily on their way again, squawking to each other like New York cab drivers. Presumably it won't be long till we get parakeet mix.

Calling a Spade a Spade

Elsewhere in the garden centre you can easily get caught up in equipment lust. We've all got perfectly functioning spades and forks and unless you're doing something Basil Fawlty-ish with them in the garden they tend to last. But when you go up to the garden centre your eye gets caught by the latest Spear and Jackson model – the Ferrari of spades – sitting gleaming on the stand, a model of robust precision engineering. The handle, like some beautifully carved wooden object d'art; the head, mirror-polished stainless steel perfection.

I may be in a minority but I think it's quite healthy to lust after garden implements. The world would surely be a better place if we all aspired to owning the best four-tined fork money could buy instead of a 60" LCD CrystalVision TV.

When I was at agricultural college I shared a house with three farmers' sons and we'd set off for college in the mornings en route to the village of Wye in Kent. Half a mile down the road and one of them would go, "Whoa! Look at that baby!" I'd spin my head round expecting them to be ogling a Maserati or an Aston Martin. But no, it would be a four-wheel drive Massey Ferguson featuring an unusual power take-off.

Get Behind Me, Satan

Apart from being able to buy stuff at garden centres, you can also go on voyages of self discovery. I've discovered I'm very mean. (That bit about buying all sorts of things when I intended to buy a 70-litre bag of multi-compost only happened the once, and, to be honest, I put the maximum/minimum thermometer back). Why buy a dibber when a pencil will do? Why buy an expensive hydrangea when you could pinch a crafty cutting, grow it yourself and have the same plant in two years' time? Why buy a propagator when you have a stock of white plastic bags from Tesco?

In fact I do have a heated propagator, but the perspex canopy broke after I dropped a flower pot on it in 1997 and the heater stopped working properly in 2001. Though it took me till 2004 to realise. Getting on for a decade later and I'm still too mean to replace it.

The propagator is like a dog that's not allowed in the

house. In spring, when I'm trying to germinate seeds, I'll sneak it into a quiet unobserved corner of the conservatory. When I get home from work I'll find my wife has placed it outside again.

At the garden centre they have a couple of beauties on sale, one that includes capillary matting, which has the slightly unnecessary description "fingertip heat control". (So what else are you going to turn the dials with, your elbows?) I come across them from time to time – whilst trying to figure out where they've moved other bits of stock – but can never justify the expense. Besides, my other one's almost new.

Ten Garden Ornaments Not to Buy Me

When it comes to the giving and receiving of presents I heartily endorse all the sentiments expressed by Ebenezer Scrooge. I especially don't want to be given plants, unless it's a house plant, which my wife can kill for me. If it's a garden plant, then if I'd wanted it I would have bought it already. But even a plant is more useful than the category of gift/insult. Rarely can you go into a shop or an area of a garden centre and say confidently that 98% of its contents is tosh. With garden ornaments you can – and I might have underestimated with that 98% figure…

Classical statuary.
An imitation Venus de Milo might look good in a showcase recreation of an Italian garden, but plonked on the edge of the patio behind a ranch-style bungalow in Thurrock is not what Michaelangelo had in mind. Worse than an exact copy is the approximate copy that's not sure if it's a tribute to the great Italian master or a Beryl Cook and has ended up like a limbless Botticelli.

Pottery meerkats.
Does my garden look like the Kalahari to you? We all love the advert. Simples. But that doesn't mean to say they're appropriate in a temperate garden. I love hippos and elephants, too.

Anthropomorphic rubbish.
A small figure of a frog, or an owl might be quite delightful in the right place in a garden. Dress that figure up in a little suit or give it a hat perched at a jaunty angle and it becomes complete and utter tat. You can buy a figurine for the garden of a mole dressed as – wait for it – a coal miner. Lovely. When your parents go out and buy something like this you know they're ready for institutional care.

Concrete wheelbarrow flower bed.
Presumably these are beloved by the same kind of people who buy limited edition ceramic plates out of Sunday supplements. A variant on this garden institution is the concrete donkey with a pannier each side acting as a flower bed. Perfect for marigolds, I'd say.

Ceramic snail.
The real ones are bad enough, but who in their right mind would want a scaled-up version? And why not have the whole set – a ceramic snail, a ceramic slug and a ceramic woodlouse?

Cat climbing out of wellington boot.
As we saw earlier, this really should be a spider.

Buddha (fat and cross-legged or less fat and recumbent).
The sight of a fat Buddha smiling from behind a clump of bamboo doesn't fill me with Zen-like calm, it fills me with un-Zen-like anger. Perhaps it might be kitsch if you could cram a Buddha, cheap bamboo water feature, model temple and stork into a little tableau for £9.99.

Smiling toadstool.
Someone must have had an LSD flashback to design this. But that still doesn't explain how they ever got to be manufactured.

Otter/squirrel cascade.
Fibreglass otters gambol next to a water cascade. From the same totally naturalistic range, three perky fibreglass squirrels perch awkwardly next to water troughs.

Hedgehog bootbrush.
Possibly the least offensive of this toxic ten. It still smacks of those tacky gift catalogues that used to sell TV dinner trays.

Grumpy Alternative Garden Ornaments

However, I wouldn't mind some of these…

1. Cat dumping in your flowerbeds or…a fox dumping on your lawn.

2. An armada of slugs of various sizes, all heading for your delphiniums.

3. A gnome rammed head-first into a wishing well.

4. Five frogs stacked on top of one another with a female at the bottom, labelled "The Optimists".

5. A playful young vixen dragging a bin-bag across the lawn.

6. Four bovver robins kicking seven shades out of a cat.

7. A rabbit dressed as Steve McQueen from *The Great Escape*, leaping a garden fence on a WWII motorbike.

8. The Beatrix Potter animals dressed up as though they'd walked straight out of *Reservoir Dogs*.

9. An animatronic snake that roams around the garden like one of those handsfree lawnmowers, scaring the screaming habdabs out of everyone.

10. An angry Little Mole with a turd on its head – straight out of the much-loved children's book.

Seeds of Doubt

We all love a good panto, but there's one panto I love more than any other. Yes, it's Jack and the Beanstalk. Oh yes it is. The concept of chucking seeds out of a window and having them germinate on the spot is one that must appeal to every gardener. Jack's mum didn't go in for endless seedbed cultivation, careful manuring, aerating, or adding compost, she just threw them out of the window. Angrily. The likelihood of anything growing that I tossed angrily onto the raised beds is about as likely as me ending up with a golden hen that sings, or going off to sea in a beautiful pea green boat. However, it's true to say that my attempts to get seeds to grow are a bit of a pantomime.

Packets of Fun

As most gardeners get to learn, there are two kinds of seed packet. There is the type that you tear open and within is a smaller, foil-enclosed packet of seeds. Then there is the type that you tear open and you suddenly realise there is no foil packet inside and you've just emptied them all out onto the path. In these situations you are forced into the humiliation of scavenging around the edges of the packet to harvest the remaining four seeds that are trapped in the joints.

Actually, there are three types of packet. The third type is the kind my wife buys for me every Christmas. Generally speaking, the illustration of the plant is more garish, the instructions simpler and the blurb on the packet will include lines such as, "Children of all ages will enjoy seeing these plants grow." She doesn't buy me wild rocket, as requested, she buys me "Zoom Zoom rocket! Salads will never be the same again!" It might have been funny the first year...

Easy Does It

When it comes to my expertise in germination, it will come as no surprise that I haven't managed to make it out of the "Easy" category listed in some seed catalogues, despite many years of gardening and membership of the RHS. If anything is listed as "Medium" I might think about giving it a try, if I was particularly keen on the plant variety; but if it is listed as "Difficult" then I don't even bother.

When I was young and carefree and felt like taking on the world I would attempt the north-west face of a packet of

Lewisia seeds. And then the second packet. And when we got to the third packet I'd realise that it was probably beyond me.* Or bamboo. I once had a packet of seeds for a particularly interesting black bamboo that I thought would look stunning in a container on the edge of the patio. When I got the planting instructions it was like a Heston Blumenthal recipe: Soak for 24 hours, then freeze, then thaw, then shake, then place in a heated propagator at between 19.5 and 19.7 degrees centigrade for two months on a vermiculite/sand mix. When germinated (ha ha ha) prick out the seedlings carefully into…well you get the drift, don't you? It wasn't going to happen.

*At this point I'd like to publicly apologise to the nice lady in Customer Services at Thompson and Morgan who kindly supplied me with the second packet of Lewisia seeds after I complained. With the clear light of hindsight it was definitely me, not the seeds.

The Inspector Poirot of Seed Trays

One of the reasons for my poor germination rate might possibly be put down to what my old physics teacher once described as "a bone idle attitude". It's one I like to think of as relaxed.

Over the years I've accumulated a variety of different seed trays – some black, some green, some brown – in an assortment of sizes. I tend to germinate four or five packets of seeds at a time. After I've planted up the five trays I have the option of writing out a plant label to identify which tray contains which. But then I think, "There's only five trays, I'll easily remember that the bush basil is in the small green tray, the sweet basil is in the large green tray, the salsify is in the brown tray, etc. No problemo. There's no need to waste a plant label."

The minute I turn my back and walk away from them, I have forgotten. A week later and there's no chance at all. And so follows the gradual plant identification as they germinate and grow and I become the Inspector Poirot of the greenhouse, finally eliminating different packets from my enquiries until I can pinpoint the suspect with certainty. It's for this same reason that one year my courgettes turned out to be the size of marrows, and my marrows turned out to be disappointingly small – almost like courgettes, in fact.

The Grumpy Ship's Botanist

It's for this reason that I hold the plant scientists at Kew in the highest of esteem. You see documentaries on television where they venture deep into the temperature-regulated vaults and bring out seeds that Sir Joseph Banks collected on one of his many plant-collecting expeditions in the eighteenth century and miraculously germinate them 200 years later.

Admittedly, they don't do it in a heated propagator that has two settings "on" and "off" (and "on" isn't guaranteed "on") with a cracked perspex lid from where a plantpot fell on it, but even so. Respect.

When Old Horace knew he had to sell up the garden centre, he had racks and racks of seeds that he couldn't return to the distributors, so they went on sale at £1 for 10 packets. I bought far too many. On the 10-year anniversary of their sell-by date (2003) I intend to celebrate the memory of Old Horace's establishment by trying to germinate some. Nobody is holding their breath.

Proper Seed Packets

Am I just imagining it or did there used to be a variety of seeds that came complete with a handy plant label? They should make this a legal requirement for all seed packets, along with a mandatory description of the difficulty involved. For me, a trip through an illustrated seed catalogue is a journey of infinite delights, tempered only by the reservation that anything I like will be too difficult to germinate. My suspicion is roused by seed packets that offer you 200 lavatera (mallow) seeds for £2. Even if only 50% of those germinated that's 100, what are you going to do with them all – open a commercial nursery? No, that must mean that they're fiendishly difficult to germinate.

What I'd like alongside the familiar abbreviations HA (Hardy Annual), HHA (Half Hardy Annual), HP (Hardy Perennial), HB (Hardy Biennial) are descriptions that will appeal to the grumpy gardener, things like GGG (Grumpy Gardener Germinatable), HGGT (Half Grumpy Gardener Tolerant) and DEGT (Don't Even Go There).

Generally speaking, the veg part of the seed catalogue is the most reliable in germination terms. If Suttons are confident that you can plant it directly into the soil then I should be able to get it to struggle into life on a cosy seed tray, nestled in seed-friendly compost, with a bit of heat applied. Beans, mangetout, broccoli, courgettes, tomatoes are all sure-fire success stories as far as I'm concerned. Even

I can't mess them up. The only valuable tip I can pass on is not to sneeze when you've just opened a £3 packet of "Sweet Olive" tomato seeds and all eight of them disappear into the atmosphere. I might stand a chance at locating a courgette seed or a bean that's been dropped, but tomatoes, forget it.

So Many Seeds, So Little Time

When I'm 65 (though it'll probably be moved to 72 by the time I get there) I know what I'm going to do. Seed catalogues make me think of retirement. You flick through page after page of fantastic plants, mentally saying "I'll have one of those, and I'll have one of those, and one of those." That bi-coloured helianthus looks amazing, stick it in the mental shopping basket, and what about some statice? You've always bought that at the florist, and, oh, look, a new double California poppy – that would be very colourful.

By the time you get to the end and reach your mental checkout, you've got about 150 packets of seeds, for which you would need a garden of about three acres. And what about the time needed to raise them? Better to wait for retirement.

Grow Your Own

So why do I struggle on and attempt to germinate seeds instead of buying a tray of plug plants at the garden centre? Well, there is just something wonderful and inspirational about starting with a humble seed packet and...saving all that money. No, I'm joking, there is something extremely satisfying about growing something splendid from seed. And then never failing to tell people how you grew that magnificent plant over there. Yes, that one over there. Oh, I told you before, did I?

There is an acacia tree in my garden that is approaching 10 feet in height (and would probably be double that if it hadn't been put in a pot), which I grew from seed and that I feel prodigiously paternalistic about.

When it comes to fertiliser time in the summer, and I have to decide which of my little beauties will benefit from the sacred elixir, it's always the acacia first. When temperatures rise and the plant pots need soaking it's always the acacia first. When I come back from holiday and check that nothing's under stress I go to the acacia first.

If trees had the capacity to hate, they would so hate that acacia. Especially the mulberry, which I really dislike, but that's another chapter.

My seed-growing Everest has to be the time I grew *Echium pininana* from seed. The best way to describe this plant is a vivid blue, 12-foot foxglove. It's a biennial from the Canary Isles, so you have to be patient and keep it away from frost in the first winter and until it starts to flower, it is singularly unimpressive. But when it sends up the dizzyingly tall blue flower spike it is a sight to behold. You don't even have to stake the thing, its stalk is so robust.

With my echium success all those years ago I thought I might have finally broken the mould and would be able to take on exciting new seed challenges, but then I read in a seed catalogue: "Another great plant for the exotic garden, *Echium pininana* is easy to grow from seed." Doh, I knew it!

Pricking Out

Once you have coaxed your seeds into life there is the next stage of pricking out.

Technically you should use a widger for this most delicate of processes, but I lost mine in about 1992. It occasionally surfaces whenever we move house, but it is the Greta Garbo of garden implements and soon retreats to the shadows. My advice to garden suppliers would be to eschew the perfectly balanced, premium price stainless-steel widger and offer a low-specification 10-pack. I'd certainly buy one of those.

In its place there is the reasonably successful plant label, or my favourite, the HB pencil. The HB pencil is longer and gives more leverage than the plant label and they are liberally scattered across the Grump household. Obviously they are not as good as a widger, but at my level of horticulture nobody is going to tell the difference.

If I were put in charge of raising seed from the last remaining Himalayan mountain flame bush then I would actually make an effort to go and find my widger.

Apart from levering out seedlings, the HB pencil can be used as a dibber, creating a hole in the seed tray or plant pot you are transferring the seedling into. To this end it is far more versatile than the plant label.

Supermarket Baggism

Another household item that is just as useful in the garden is the supermarket bag. I am a big fan of the Tesco bag. Instead of inserting a tray of seeds or seedlings into a propagator, where you have to be mindful of direct sunlight, you can use a Tesco bag. Because they are white, Grump science tells me they will allow some sunlight through and reflect that around once it's inside. The Waitrose bag is just as good, but if we could afford to shop there regularly we wouldn't have to grow our own vegetables. The Sainsbury's bag, being orange, is better for seedlings that have come on a bit, which you want to protect from strong sunlight.

Calamity. Recently I've been going into Tesco and they've been handing out blue bags. This is either an interruption of supply or the shape of things to come. By the time this book hits the shelves the blue Tesco bag might have become the grey squirrel at the checkout, wrecking my spring planting agenda. Only time will tell.

Arthur C. Grump's Great Mysteries of the Seed World

How are they so blinking sure that there are 1,500 seeds in a lettuce packet? They can't count them, do they weigh them instead? Lettuce seeds are like fairy dust, you need something like a mass spectrometer to work out how much they weigh. I'm not so mean that I'm going to start counting them, I'm just curious.

To be fair, if they're precious F1 tomatoes and you only get 10, I do count them.

And I'm not ashamed, the top varieties can work out at about 30p a seed. You wouldn't go into a newsagent and have the guy behind the counter say – "That's £2.60 change or it might be £2.30, or it might be £2, anyway it's somewhere around that."

And while we're on about seed numbers; why do seed companies offer you 180 or 190 of a certain seed? Why not make it 150 or 200. Having decided the variety that suits you best you're hardly going to be swayed by those extra 30 seeds.

* I once saw bonsai seed advertised for sale. What is the point of bonsai seed? Is it tiny, tiny seed, in a tiny, tiny packet – like a big packet but scaled down really small? Does it come in its own rack, which is five inches tall?

Learn Your Lesson Grump!

It's taken me many years to learn this, but if I can pass on this one tip about seed germination all my work here won't have been in vain.

I once tried to germinate some Chinese lantern seeds. I followed the sowing instructions on the packet carefully, covered the seeds with a quarter of an inch of compost, slipped the seed tray inside my standard Tesco bag and put it into the greenhouse. I got nothing for three weeks. Finally one miserable Chinese Lantern seedling in the corner of the tray popped its head up to the world. I waited another two weeks. Nothing else. And so I tended my sole survivor like any loving parent would, transferring it to a small pot and then a larger pot. I proudly showed my father-in-law. He said "that's not a Chinese Lantern, that's a weed". I looked closer. It was a weed.

I'd taken old compost from another seed tray which had been contaminated and the only thing prepared to grow in it was a volunteer. The lesson is: always use new seed compost if you don't know what your seedlings are going to look like.

Bulbs

Bulbs are far less of a challenge than seeds but they're still something to worry about. Don't assume that because they are big and bulky that they can look after themselves. Various pests in the garden view them as an all-you-can-eat bargain bucket. I'm presuming that's what happened to my snowdrops in the winter of 2009. The two most hated months of the year are January and February, so I thought what better way to hasten spring than have a bank of snowdrops (all right, a small mound of snowdrops, our garden isn't big enough for a bank). I went down to the garden centre and bought myself a pack of 50, yes 50, snowdrop bulbs.

The following January I got two sets of leaves and one flower. One miserable solitary blinking flower! That's the god's honest truth. Bring me a copy of the *RHS Garden Encyclopedia* – aka the bible – and I'll put my right hand on it and swear an oath.

I'm sure if I'd have put my ear close to the ground, all I would have heard was the sound of slugs belching.

Grump's Law of Bulb Survival

Grump's Law of Bulb Survival states that the more you pay for a particularly beautiful bulb, the more slugs and snails will seek it out and destroy it. At the same time, the plainest bulbs in your garden, the miserable dullards that lose their petals the second the wind rises above a gentle zephyr, that you've half a mind to hoik out and start again, will go on flourishing from year to year.

Nature is perverse like this. In Africa, on the great plains of the Serengeti, the weakest wildebeest gets picked off by the packs of lions and hyenas. In the grumpy garden, the failing, sickly blind daffodils get left alone. Billy Joel was clearly a grumpy gardener when he sang, "Only the Good Die Young". Those are my bulbs he's singing about.

Jobs to Avoid in March

Spring is when all hell breaks loose in the garden and you are expected to perform a whole range of chores, most of which you have managed successfully to put off for most of the winter. March is a time when they become inevitable, however to offset this, you need to make sure the friendly gardening journal, with its Tasks For March column doesn't land you with any more jobs than you need take on. Trust me. Most of it can be carried forward to April – and to be honest, the journal doesn't know what part of the country you live in. March in Surrey is still February in Darlington.

Divide congested clumps of Snowdrops while still in leaf.
That's if you can find them.

Dig out and divide hostas. And disturb froggy?
I much prefer the frogs in the hostas than in the pond so they're staying put. Also, like so many of the plants I'm exhorted to divide, I have nowhere to put them when they're divided. Maybe if they started a web site for lonely divided perennials we could set about matching up the plants who didn't have a garden with ardent gardeners.

Take the old flower heads off winter flowering heathers.
I prefer a managed burn, a little like the grouse moors of Scotland. And it does make my neighbour, Mrs MacDonald misty eyed and reminiscent of when she was roaming in the gloaming (and I suspect she did a lot of roaming, whether it was gloaming or not).

Help flower pollination of open blossoms by dabbing them with a soft paintbrush.
That sounds like a job creation scheme for young offenders sent on community service. How much time would you need to have on your hands to go round doing this?

Check greenhouse plants and new shoots outdoors for signs of aphids.
The No.1 sign for me being an aphid sat on the shoot looking up at me with an air of trepidation in its compound eye.

Lift, divide and replant chives in a sunny position.
My chives are fine where they are, thank you and they don't need to go on holiday. This is tantamount to accusing you of

planting them in a stupid place. If they got big enough to form a whole clump in the first place I would assume they were in the right place to start off with!

Spray peach trees to help control peach leaf curl.
That's all very well if you've got a sprayer whose nozzle doesn't block the moment you put anything other than water through it and a dry, calm weekend day to spray it on. I tried this once in a moderate breeze and made myself thoroughly resistant to peach leaf curl and a variety of mildews, including thrips. I'm not sure if even 15% of it went on the tree.

Clean your greenhouse windows to ensure plants and seedlings get maximum light.
I'm a devotee of the Quentin Crisp school of housework which states that after two years it doesn't get much worse. Surely allowing rain to clean the window pains is the most eco-friendly way and in many ways I am the epitome of an eco warrior. All right, I've got some old corduroys.

Ventilate greenhouses well on sunny days or the temperature will soar.
In March you leave the house at 7am when it's virtually freezing, so you can hardly open the windows then. Even if you do decide to risk it and open them, sod's law will dictate that you only remember to shut the windows again the following Tuesday.

It isn't too late to improve heavy clay soils for better yields.
Too right, there's always next year when you won't have so much on.

Make a diary of spring-flowering bulbs for a year-by-year comparison of tulips, daffodils and others.
Right, well that's not going to happen.

Garden Pests

It may be "the circle of life" and all that baloney, but it gets on my nerves. We all know how ecology works; plant grows, bug eats plant, bigger bug eats smaller bug, reptile eats bigger bug, mammal eats reptile, man comes out of conservatory shouting angrily at mammal to get out of his ****ing garden.

Gardening would be so much more pleasurable if it weren't for the fauna. Okay, maybe the occasional bee would be allowed in and yes, the worms would already be in the ground so we don't need to exclude them, plus it would be fine for the friendly robin to come bob bob bobbing along. But everything else – no, you're barred.

Sadly life isn't like this and you have to put up with…

Slugs

I blame Noah. He could have whipped up that gang plank long before the two slugs got onto the Ark and we wouldn't have had slug trails all over the garden. What are they for anyway? We don't need them to eat lots of decomposing vegetable matter because the worms can do that. The only thing they seem to be good for is feeding to hedgehogs and, bizarrely, koi carp seem to like them too.

Certainly if I needed to get a job as a gourmet chef catering for slugs then I have the perfect c.v. – my choice of vegetable crop is always a delight to them. Rarely do I grow anything that doesn't meet with their wholehearted approval.

Unlike every right-on garden programme I seem to watch, I have no compunction in getting out the big tube of slug pellets and administering death generously. If anyone wants to complain then I'd like to point out that it's the circle of life and I'm a predator. It seems to me that the way television gardeners deal with slugs is just to dodge the issue, to repel them a little bit so they're just off camera.

Having talked the macho slug termination talk I have to confess that the only slugs I take direct action with are ones I find munching my plants. These are not killed *per se*, they are sent to the Guantanamo Bay of slugs – Mrs MacDonald's yew tree – via an aerial route. It's not killing them, it's giving them something a bit more challenging to try.

Taking a slug

The garden programmes are not alone in getting a bit squeamish about disposing of the slug menace. There are a number of products you can buy at the garden centre that pussyfoot around the whole death-to-slugs issue. One of these is slug blocker granules. You don't harm the slugs, you give them a chemical Keep Out notice by surrounding your favourite plants with it. So basically you're fobbing them off without incurring slug-slaughter guilt.

On the same lines, you can purchase slug stoppa metal tape to wind round your prize plants to stop slugs shimmying up the outside of pots. Great for protecting individual plants, not so good for a raised bed.

And there is a dimension that the manufacturers might not have thought about. Both products might be counter productive by inciting slug rage. Like teenagers denied entry to city centre nightclubs they could be so infuriated by slug stoppa granules that an army of vengeful slugs set about every stalk and leaf they can get hold of in a plant-killing slug-rampage frenzy. It's a thought.

Nematode Hall

One way of killing slugs without using nasty chemicals is to opt for a biological control. These days you can send away for 12 million nematodes by post to replicate what the pellets would do. These little devils, when watered into the ground, will seek out slugs and penetrate their bodies causing the slugs to stop eating and die within a week. As my daughter would say; "awesome". It's an organic solution which will satisfy the bearded sandal-wearers out there, and not just the women, the men too.

But it's a much slower death than most slug pellets produce. The chemical in the pellet causes the slugs to over-produce mucus until they die of dehydration. Aaawww.

Nematodes can also be used on vine weevil, chafer grubs, leather jackets, codling moths and ants, which aren't killed by the nematodes, they just hate them and will relocate. Codling moth caterpillars don't fare so well.

I have to say, I like the sound of them, especially as the company that produces them is called Nemesys, which must be the singular most brilliant name for a garden supply company ever. (All we need now is a little wooden house for them and we can call it a Nematode-itat).

All Mouth and No Squashing

Now, I have a confession to make. On a rainy night if I meet a slug out in the garden crossing a path I don't kill it for having the temerity to be in my garden. If they're out and about as a slug in transit, fair enough. What I might do, if I find one lurking suspiciously underneath a plant pot, is pick it up and place it where it is a little more exposed to a natural predator. Our 17-foot-wide trampoline is the perfect venue for the challenge that has been dubbed "The Slug Gauntlet". You simply lob the slug into the centre and if it manages to make it to the edge without being pounced upon by a bird then it wins its freedom. Admittedly the kids aren't that keen on having their trampoline covered in slug trails, (and it's better to do it when they're not bouncing around on it) but the rain soon washes the trails off.

'Hence from Verona art thou banished!'

Snails get a slightly different treatment to slugs. You might even say there's a certain apartheid that operates in my back garden when it comes to *Mollusca domestica*. Instead of being hurled to a remote place, they are dealt a Shakespearian fate. They are banished.

We have a council-run brown bin service where gardeners can buy a brown-topped wheelie bin and fill it with garden waste which they will empty every two weeks. It's normally the repository for weeds and trimmed branches, cut-down stems and grass cuttings.

Snails are banished to the challenging environment of the brown bin and thence...who knows where. It's a little like transporting cockney criminals to Australia.

Of course it would be good if Hugh Fearnley-Whittingstall could come up with a delicious recipe that makes the most of this plentiful resource – maybe put it in a book and call it *River Cottage Eats The Garden*. Hugh's normal method for eating something unpalatable is to stick some butter, some garlic, some onions, some chopped bacon and a bit of seasoning into a pan and then add the unspeakable thing. Snails would probably fit into this template. The liner from my wellington boots would probably fit into this template, too.

Children

Young primates, otherwise known as children, are the single biggest pest in the garden. They might not eat as much plant matter or ringbark trees the way Muntjac deer do, but you know they've passed through. Your own children soon learn that picking mummy a nice bunch of flowers from the ones in the garden might be fun on *Teletubbies,* but it makes daddy go purple and emit steam.

They also learn quickly that using plantpots for goalposts makes daddy say very rude words and threaten to put teddy through the garden shredder. It's a boundaries thing.

Jean Paul Sartre said that "hell is other people". It's not, hell is other people's children.

The trouble in the garden starts when your friends come over with their youngsters and they have a more laissez faire attitude to child supervision. All of a sudden you find that kids are stomping through your flowerbeds, flattening the daffodils and tulips and treading on the emerging sedum heads.

They are throwing stuff in the pond to try and get the attention of the goldfish who are cowering at the bottom. They try and climb up your clematis obelisk, knock stuff over and run amok. All the while you sit there with a stiffening jaw, pretending to be listening to your friends talking, with a steadily clenched fist round your glass of dry white wine.

When it finally becomes all too much for you and you shout "Don't DO that!" you get treated like you're the Child Catcher from *Chitty Chitty Bang Bang* – "they're only having a little game!"

It's at times like these that I wish we could be having the

return visit straight away. I'd make sure my children were all equipped with felt pens when we went round to their house and they could go and draw all over their wallpaper – at which point I'd say, "they're only drawing a little picture…"

Ah, the Little Treasures

And it can ruin friendships you've enjoyed for years. Right-minded people who you have a lot of affection for come to your garden and their children treat it like it was a municipal space. A friend of my wife's was round and let her four-year-old wander off down the garden.

You all know how much space pumpkins take up. I had decided to give over a chunk of the precious veg patch to growing three pumpkins. Some indeterminate animal, probably a fox, had dug up one and killed it after six weeks so I was down to two. All of a sudden junior comes round the corner holding one of the remaining two pumpkins, which at that stage was about the size of an orange.

"Oh clever boy," said his mum encouragingly, "what have you found…?"

There was no hint of an apology. All I got was, "how was he supposed to know he shouldn't pick it?"

He was supposed to know because you were supposed to blinking well teach him.

She didn't take my offer to create a little chicken-wire play coop for him as a joke. Sadly she *has* been back since.

Grumpy, and Then Some

It's rare that I can be outgrumped, but my brother-in-law – let's call him Michael – surpasses even me in the grumpy stakes. Although I have become like Old Horace in my dealings with children, he takes it a stage further. He gets grumpy when children simply walk on his grass. This doesn't leave a great deal of room for manoeuvre for his children who are confined to playing on a two-foot wide, 30-foot long concrete path between his house and his shed. I could understand it if it was an amazing verdant carpet straight out of a lawn seed advert, with a rare mix of exotic fescues, but no. It's just grass. I told him he should get out more but of course that would be impossible, who would be at home to look after the lawn?

Cats

I think if I were more successful at attracting nesting birds into the garden I'd be more twitchy about cats. As it is we get the occasional state visit from Jasper, the feckless cat from next door who thinks he's rather special, but has nothing to back up this claim. Whenever we see him he's loping about like a teenager in the middle of some emotional crisis – everything is too much effort. He would make a great emo.

He seems to be useless at catching anything other than voles with Zimmer frames or mice that run headlong into his paws. Even then he's not so sure what his next move would be. When he was younger he used to sit at the edge of the pond gazing at the fish, but he's given that up. He's probably calculated that if he fell in the pond, the fish would mug him.

He occasionally graces us with a toilet stop in the raised beds but there's no pungent cat marking. While some gardens are at the confluence of several cat territories and the flowerbeds become the walls on which cat gangs leave foul-smelling graffiti, ours seems to be like No Man's Land, patrolled by a foppish cat who's only motivation is to get back in time for the next meal.

The Perfect All-Grumpy Deterrent

Our friend Julia has a real problem with cats in the front garden and has installed one of those infra-red-activated water jet deterrents. This can be used on any large pest in the garden and sends out a jet of water the moment it detects motion nearby. The only problem comes when she needs to go out of the house and has to take a circuitous route affecting a limbo-dancing motion to get into the car and avoid getting soaked. She says it was a great surprise to the postman.

From a general grumpy point of view these would be marvellous installed in any front garden to prevent people from posting endless pizza delivery leaflets through your front door, or positioned around your vegetable patch to deter small children.

Squirrels

There have been quite a few natural history programmes on television showing how amazingly intelligent squirrels are at solving problems in their bid to get at nuts. All I can say is they must have contacted their local MENSA Squirrels branch to find their volunteers because the ones in my garden are as thick as two short planks.

My lawn is full of little squirrel scrapes where they come back looking for things they think they've planted. They dig out the compost in my seedling pots and I know for certain that there is nothing of nutritional interest in there.

When they run away, they run away stupidly. I once cycled into the alley near our house and caught one on the ground just by the entrance. The alley has a six-foot fence either side so it raced the whole 200 metres down to the other end to escape me, rather than, stop, turn round and let me ride past. It was very funny, though. It was like one of the training sequences from *Rocky*, me cycling side by side with a squirrel, putting it through its paces.

As Tested by Squirrels

Their presence in gardens has spawned a whole new level of heavy duty bird feeders that advertise themselves as "bite resistant" but don't claim to be squirrel proof. The ones that do boast that quality on the label are intricate contraptions that have a series of bars preventing the squirrel getting close to the central nut chamber, like it was the Hannibal Lecter of the garden.

They're like a cross between an experimental art structure

82

from the 1950s and a school metalwork project that's gone badly wrong.

The best squirrel-proof nut dispenser of all, though, is the one that spins round. If you thought Wallace and Gromit didn't invent anything you can buy in the shops, think again. This crafty device consists of a motorised housing, under which hangs a conventional bird feeder. When the squirrels jump onto the housing above in preparation for swinging down and getting the nuts below, the weight-sensitive housing starts spinning round throwing the squirrel to the ground.

It's like *Total Wipeout* for squirrels. I am sorely tempted…

Foxes

I think you know I hate foxes. As far as I am concerned they are Garden Enemy No.1. They come into the garden and dig huge holes for no reason, they poop all over the lawn, they poop on the patio, on the paths, on the drive, and they are no respecter of a man's wellingtons.

They'll try and eat anything you leave out. I've got teethmarks in my Nishi-Koi fish food tub where it's tried to pick up the thing and make off with it in its jaws. Compared to the physical damage done by slugs or snails, or the birds stealing ripe cherries, or wasps and codling moths burrowing into the apples, their impact is limited. All it boils down to is an ongoing dirty protest. But it is irritating as hell. And while the heron gets me angry too, at least it has the bottle to fly into the garden in broad daylight and not sneak under the fence in the middle of the night.

Spiders

Spiders are only a pest in the garden when it comes to the autumn and even then they're just a comedy pest. You can be walking down a path on a crisp autumn morning when splat – your face becomes enmeshed in a cobweb strung up overnight by an autumn spider. These are fat, quite beautiful spiders and you feel loathe to destroy what they've done, except for the fact that they've constructed a web between the spade you left stuck in the ground and the fence. (I am a believer in the free-range garden tool and often have several spades at strategic places in the garden).

But I dislike the fat black beefsteak spiders that inhabit the bottom of a stack of plantpots, especially when they start running towards you as though you were an arachnophile not a 'phobe.

Caterpillars

Throughout the UK there are national collections of plants. I've visited the wonderful Picton Gardens on the other side of the Malvern Hills to see their National Collection of Michaelmas Daisies, a wall of vivid purples, lilacs and mauves and every shade thereof, from September through to October.

In my garden I have the national collection of brassica-eating caterpillars. Any time I think of growing cabbages, or something a bit similar, they come down on them in their Genghis Khan-like larvae hordes. Savoy cabbages? Oooh yum. How about some sprouts? Yep, they'll do.

Such was the pestilential infestation in my garden that I

thought, "right you devils, a plague on your house" and steadfastly refused to plant them for five years. Then my head was turned by a tray of purple sprouting broccoli plants I saw at the garden centre and relented. Once planted they grew prodigiously quickly. And no sign of caterpillars whatsoever. The moment they started to show signs of bolting I whipped them out faster than you can say *BBC Sound Effects Volume 1*. (All the classic horror film sound effects were created with cabbages – the sound of guillotines, choppers and a neck being twisted and broken, it's all cabbages).

But just as with all good horror films there was a sting in the tail. It was a Sunday evening and we had just enjoyed a delicious roast with the sprouting broccoli when my wife took a closer look at the spare stalks she was putting back in the fridge. Deep in the axils of the plant there were a lot of tiny, just emerged caterpillars. We hadn't noticed.

To be honest they wouldn't have survived the boiling and we didn't tell the kids…

Wasps

As with slugs, what are wasps for? If you are a believer in creationist theory you've got to question the big man's thinking on this one. He already had small birds, lacewings and ladybirds to predate aphids, what did he need wasps for? Did he suspect that man would move on from the Adam and Eve stage and eventually invent the afternoon tea. And just in case he got a bit too complacent he'd create wasps to cause a bit of bother in the jam area?

And here's another poser – were there wasps in the

Garden of Eden? Given the amount of protective clothing that was supplied by the Almighty, I'm sure Adam and Eve would have a very good case to prosecute him under Health and Safety legislation.

'Let Me Through, I'm a Beekeeper!'

My hatred for wasps is exacerbated by the fact that they drive bees to distraction in the autumn. From August onwards they try and get into hives to rob them of honey. Any wasps that get in past the guards at the entrance have to be pursued round the hive, caught and dispatched. It's a time-consuming occupation for the bees which have better things to do at that time of year, i.e. make me honey.

When you take the roof off a hive, the effective ceiling of the hive is called a crown board. These come in glass or wood. Some beekeepers don't like the glass ones because they can cause condensation, but they do allow you to look inside to see what's going on. In the autumn, you open up and there's usually some game of "wasp chase" going on. One wasp followed by about six or seven workers.

To make it easier for the bees to protect their home at this time of year, beekeepers will narrow the entrance from the full width of the hive to a small gap. That allows the sentries to be a bit more vigilant, but still wasps get in. In fact the signs of a failing colony are its inability to defend its entrance properly.

The good news is that bees can sting wasps without losing their stingers, whereas they would if they stung you or me. But particularly me. Our rough epidermis means they can't get it back.

Because I'm used to being stung on a regular basis I have no fear of wasps and enjoy a bit of *mano a waspo* on a late summer afternoon.

Moles

When I was at college in, as we have established, "the olden days", we rented a gate cottage off a modest Victorian house. One of the provisos of our cheap student stay was that we maintained the garden for the old lady who lived there on her own. But it was surely going to be a doddle for three Agriculture and one Rural Studies students.

We lopped and chopped the mature shrubs in a rudimentary fashion, mowed the lawn with an old Suffolk Punch petrol mower and our tenure at what we dubbed 'The Bolthole' seemed to be going okay. Until the moles arrived. "We had the moles in 1954," Mrs Atkinson informed us with great precision, but she couldn't remember how her gardener had got rid of them.

We Tried Everything

Poisoned worms dropped into their tunnels didn't seem to work, nor mole smokers that produced deadly purple cyanide gas. The traps we put out were skilfully bypassed.

Robin, who was in the gun club and had his own shotgun, sat out one night and was going to shoot when he saw them pushing earth up, but fell asleep. To be honest, it wasn't the greatest idea either, having a trigger happy, semi-comatose student in your garden.

After exams in June Mrs Atkinson went to visit her sister and we had the most fabulous, hard rocking party out in the garden that stretched from Saturday lunchtime till the police arrived in the early hours of Sunday morning.

In that time we went through the greatest hits of the Stones, Status Quo, Led Zeppelin, Dire Straits, Deep Purple, Be Bop Deluxe, the Stranglers, you name it, it got played twice. There was dancing, singing, drinking and the mad anarchistic things that agriculture students like to do such as midnight croquet.

That was enough for the moles. After the party they never produced another molehill. Not in our garden anyway. It probably wasn't the choice of music that did it but the constant pounding of footsteps backwards and forwards across the lawn for this most vibration sensitive of animals.

Pond Life

When we moved into our present house, it came complete with a reasonably large pond, something I'd always wanted. Over the years, *Gardener's World* had run endless features on rushes and sedges and bog marginal plants and I'd looked on enviously and thought, "one day…" It was never going to be an option when you have young children because we've all seen the film *Don't Look Now* and knew for certain that the moment our back was turned they'd be a kersplosh!

When the day arrived that I could have my own pond I realised, to my consternation, that they actually involved work. You see my idealised pond, probably gleaned from watching *Bambi* as a child, was a sylvan, moss-edged watering hole, full of crystal clear water with languid goldfish or koi gliding beneath the surface of the water, while overhead dragon and damsel flies hovered, swooped and hovered again. Frogs would croak playfully and splash into the water.

In reality the frogs treated my pond more as a love hotel, a quick five minutes and they were gone. When it wasn't covered with duckweed it was obliterated by algae. When I managed to get rid of both with very expensive treatments, the heron got a clear view of the goldfish and made short work of them. Then we went on holiday and the duckweed came back, and then the algae came back, and I got rid of both again with more expensive chemicals that wouldn't kill the water lilies; then the heron came back and took the remaining goldfish that it hadn't got the first time.

Joy.

Heron Wars

And then I thought I'm not giving in to the damned heron and bought some more goldfish and a net to cover the pond. Which ruins any kind of aesthetic effect that the pond might bring to your garden, but it's a sure-fire way of hanging on to your livestock.

A well-meaning neighbour from across the road suggested that if I dig the pond to a certain depth, then herons wouldn't be able to stand up and wade around and the fish would be safe. His koi were perfectly safe and his pond was net-free.

My pond was already losing water through the summer months so I thought this might be the perfect opportunity to replace the liner, dig it out much deeper and two fingers to the heron.

Digging out big chunks of London clay wasn't the most fun I've had with my wellingtons on but after two days of back-straining excavation and muddy boot trails everywhere across the garden, the new frog leisure pool and love hotel was complete. The rubberised pond liner was installed, this time complete with fountain, and I started to fill it with water.

My neighbour had kindly kept my old water lilies in the corner of his pond while I was burrowing a new one but he was out when I went over the road to get them back. His wife showed me through to the back. Looking round, I couldn't see any koi in his pond at all. "Oh," said his wife, "the heron got them…"

Rustle Up the Crow

As you can imagine I wasn't wholly confident that the deeper pond was going to do the business at warding off the heron so I made the mistake that many pond keepers do. I bought a dummy plastic heron.

Now your average garden robin might be ultra-territorial, even challenging its own reflection in garden mirrors to a bit of birdy fisticuffs, but it turns out that herons are a bit more chilled than that. My dummy heron must have been a sexy lady heron because it soon caught the eye of other male herons. In a way it was like a signpost that said, "Hey, they've got loads of fish down here!" or "Look how still I can stand, there's obviously nobody in the garden to disturb me!" and a heron soon returned to take three mirror carp.

A much better idea to keep the herons at bay is to involve your local crows. If crows are in the area and the heron alights on one of our nearby roofs, the crows will soon move it on. A couple of the young delinquent crows will try and pick a fight, flying above it and forcing it to fend them off with that big, fish-loving beak. In the end it gets so weary it flaps off.

I like crows.

Maybe they should sell dummy plastic crows in the garden supply catalogues and I could put them by the pond instead.

Waterboatmen

Goldfish can be very annoying too. If they get scared they will skulk at the bottom of the pond for weeks on end, refusing to come to the surface, like sulky teenagers holing out in their bedroom. I only realised this after I had dug out my new pond and placed bamboo carefully across it instead of a net.

I came home from work one day to find my second batch of goldfish had disappeared entirely. I couldn't quite work out how the heron had got round the bamboo, (and taken ALL of them) but clearly it had, because no fish were to be seen for the next two weeks. I finally gave in to the inevitable and went down to the fish shop and pretended I needed some more, rather than confess to the fact that I was now the fishmonger to our local wading birds.

When I got back to the garden, surprise surprise, my goldfish had decided to put in an appearance again, if only to welcome six more into their ranks. All this stuff about them having a memory of fifteen seconds is wrong, they clearly felt mortally offended for two weeks. Unless they got down to the bottom of the pond and couldn't remember why they'd gone there.

Half of me thinks I should allow nature to take its course and learn to love the pond-skimmers and waterboatmen. They demand no maintenance and have a happy time of it. And I do see them from time to time, unlike my piscatorial teenagers who surface for food then go back to their bedrooms for a sulk.

Eco-Friendly or Eco-Grumpy...

After my second pond pump failed in as many years I decided to further enhance my green credentials. To solve the twin problems of not enough oxygen in the water and too much algae, and following careful research on the internet, I plumped for some algae-eating water snails, some oxygenating plants and a solar-powered aerator. I was so green I was almost Irish.

For those who have stuck their toes in the water of renewable energy by investing in solar-powered garden lights…you probably know what's coming.

I diligently set up my pond aerator with the solar capture panel (about as big as a magazine) optimised in full sunlight. And waited. And waited and waited and waited. Nada. Nothing. Not a single bubble did it produce. It was about as much use as a dummy plastic heron in a heron scaring contest.

I'd always thought that the dim glow – calling it a light is surely contravening the trades description act – that solar garden 'lights' produced was down to the small size of the panel. This was a big panel, yet still it was absolutely useless.

I never saw my algae-loving snails again either. They didn't go off and breed like rabbits, they just went off. A few years later when I was emptying the pond I found a single shell and that was it. They did a Lord Lucan on me. The oxygenating plants sank too far into the pond and presumably didn't get enough sunlight and died. Nature's a wonderful thing when I'm assisting.

The Mating Instinct

The water snails might not be particularly impressed with my pond, but try telling that to the frogs. And I do mean the amphibians here, not the nation. Though, come to think of it, they do both like snails.

These days I protect my pond fish from the heron with a framework of interlaced bamboo sticks which make it very difficult to wade about. In the autumn, the bamboo lattice comes off and the net comes back on. I'll put stones on top of the net all the way round so that the frogs can't get in and lay frogspawn in the spring which the fish will simply eat at their leisure. It's for their own good.

Given the security arrangements I've put in place I'm utterly amazed to find that by the middle of March there's frogspawn in the pond. How do they get in there? There's no sign of where they got in yet there's the result glistening on the surface on a bright spring morning. Surely they don't creep in there in September and overwinter in the sludge at the bottom? Maybe October or November, but September? That's the froggy equivalent of putting the towel down on the sun lounger even before the Germans get there!

People say that squirrels are smart but frogs must have an

entire committee planning ways of getting into my pond.

Typically there's a few stupid ones too who jump onto the net like it was a frog-poline and I have to spend hours disentangling the resulting spawn from the net. Although this is probably a diversionary tactic and while I'm getting the slippery gloop off my hands they're all piling into the pond at the other end.

The Ponder Years

We shuffle about this mortal coil for only a brief second in the life of the planet, but traces of our presence will live on across the years. Many plants and creatures lived, died and their remains fell to the bottom of the great Jurassic seas where they were compressed and fossilised into sedimentary rocks.

A hundred millions years from now a geologist of the future may come across what has lived, died or fallen to the bottom of my pond. It will be a varied set of fossils, but I think it will give an interesting insight into how homo sapiens were surviving out in the suburbs.

There'll be a few mirror carp skeletons, water snail shells, at least one screwdriver, bits of wire, the odd plant label, an ice cream wrapper or two and a range of discarded fountain heads that didn't give the kind of spray effect pictured on the box.

...On a Little Dishee, When The Heron Comes In

One way of making a heron think about coming onto the Grump estate – and I'll actually make it one of these days – is the concrete goldfish. What I'd do is this. Make a concrete model of a goldfish, paint it goldy red and stick it on a spike about 15 centimetres under the surface of the pond in amongst the lillies...and then wait for the heron to arrive. You know that might take a lot of swallowing. If it can get past the bent beak.

Vegetable Man

Children say the funniest things don't they. They also make you very proud. My daughter has played recorder in the school band (sometimes known as the sound torture experiment project). She's been in the school netball team, performed sports acrobatics for her club, but one of her finest moments was when she went round to a friend's house for tea and was given burger and chips. She looked at the plate and said, "Where are the vegetables then?" That's my girl. Sadly they're not to be found in my garden...

'We've Got an Allotment!'

About fifteen years ago I considered getting an allotment. In those days it wasn't trendy and there was easily a plot to be had if you wanted one. Back then food wasn't as wallet-numbingly expensive as it is today and a carbon footprint was something you got from walking through coal. And people would have laughed if you talked about worries over your food mileage.

I can't claim to be a veg visionary, I didn't particularly want to grow vegetables on my little square of land. First and foremost it was going to be the repository for my two hives and maybe a few kiwi fruit vines as well.

Things have changed since then and the vegetable patch is no longer the Cinderella area of the garden and at dinner parties there is talk of "what are you growing this year?" What I can't stand, though, are the people who've suddenly got an allotment and isn't growing your own veg fantastic.

These are people who have a garden already, but don't want to turn it over to fruit and veg production. So they drive backwards and forwards to the allotment in their gas guzzling 4x4 or MPV using excess fuel and resources just to be able to say they've got an allotment and they're doing their bit.

"It's something we can do together and the kids love it too!" Do they hell. Children and vegetables hate each other, unless it's chips or the pumpkin they're about to hollow out for Halloween. Or my daughter.

In the Grump Republic nobody would be allowed an allotment who had a car that was less than five years old and mentioning that you had one would be a treasonable offence.

Better To Say Nothing

Fancy a spectacular new blackberry? (And we're not talking about that stupid mobile phone for people with tiny fingers). Would you be interested in a variety producing large berries as big as a tayberry, superbly flavoured, early fruiting and producing massive crops? I did too, so I sent away for one and it wasn't cheap – about £12 as I remember. Yes, for a blackberry! You could probably get the mobile phone cheaper these days.

If that wasn't crazy enough imagine the laughs I had when I came back and discovered that my wife had removed "that bramble that was stuck at the end of the raspberries. I'm surprised you didn't see it…"

Le Terroir des Legumes

The French have this thing they call *terroir*, a combination of soil and climate which makes one patch of ground distinctly different for growing grapes than another. I was never convinced about this until Oz and James did France in their series on BBC2. Genial wine buff Oz Clarke was able to demonstrate to the very sceptical James May from *Top Gear* the difference between two bottles of wine grown on vineyards across the road from each other.

This was good news as far as I was concerned because it reinforced my view that the *terroir* for producing *legumes* at *Chateau Grump* was unique. In effect it was the perfect get-out clause. As I'm always telling Leaf Lady, "zis clay soil, he is always so tough for ze tendere vegetables!"

Not Just Petites Pois

My own particular *terroir* is less than ideal for producing large vegetables. It is very well suited for producing small ones. Now that would probably have been an issue for men in the garden a few years ago, but now that Marks and Spencer and Waitrose are selling packs of mini veg, and they are available in swanky restaurants, mini veg are particularly hip.

Whereas commercial market gardeners will harvest their normal-sized veg early, I prefer to adopt the technique used by livestock farmers who place a premium on how long their beef takes to mature and grow. My mini veg takes just as long to grow as normal size veg would take. Except mine never struggle above the mini size.

I grew some carrots once and after a season in the ground they came out looking suitable for a dolls' house kitchen. Perfectly shaped, mind you, none of the *That's Life* suggestive knobbles to them, just consistently very small.

The Bristlecone Pine of Leeks

One of the fascinating side aspects of my *terroir* is the length of time something can stay in the ground. In the spring before Old Horace closed up his garden centre for good I bought a tray of leek seedlings by the checkout. I love leeks and I'd never grown them in the garden before so, why not.

I planted them and they seemed happy enough – the right colour, not being ravaged by insect larvae, not fallen over, minding their own business. Every so often I would check back to see what the progress was and you'd have to describe it as tardy. By the autumn, when I should have been harvesting them, they weren't a whole lot bigger than when they started off.

Horace's garden centre closed and the site was boarded up. A year passed. The leeks started to hit their stride in the second year and began to look more like spring onions. They certainly weren't the size of the leeks I'd hoed while working on a farm near Boston in Lincolnshire when I was a student, but he'd probably used loads of fertiliser.

By the autumn, my biennial leeks were still on the small size and these were the days before I came to terms with mini veg, so I left them be.

The third year was very exciting because they started to build a sumptuous new garden centre on the site of Old Horace's place. The leeks struggled on. A friend who was looking round the garden noticed the row and said, "you're growing leeks again." I said nothing. I saw a programme about horticultural clubs who grew monster veg and one of the items was about the intensive competition between different leek growers. How can they get a leek that big?

It was in the autumn of the third year whilst buying three bags of bark mulch at the new garden centre that it suddenly hit home to me, my leeks were actually older than this enterprise.

Counting the (Onion) Rings

Enough was enough, I had to harvest them. They were still not very big, and though they had become quasi-ornamental, and a bit of a novelty, their function was to be eaten. I was still quite surprised that they hadn't gone to seed, but now was the time. Would they taste like leeks or would they taste like very old and woody Great Basin bristlecone pines?

They tasted fine. I haven't grown leeks again, though.*

*For domestic harmony reasons I asked my wife to review the text before I submitted it and she said it was four years, not three. But, what dolt would leave a leek in the ground for four years...?

Organic or Cheapskate?

I'm sure someone with a beard and a llama wool jumper, driving a sunflower-oil-powered Morris Traveller has worked out the definition of organic seed, but if you want my two penn'th, it's a load of old claptrap.

The reason for my scepticism about tagging the word organic onto anything is that I once saw some honey advertised as "organic honey". How can the producers be sure that the bees only visited flowers that were pesticide free? The answer is they can't.

And as far as I know there is no effective organic treatment for the tracheal mite varroa which is decimating bee colonies across the United Kingdom, you have to bring in chemical assistance. This is done after the honey has been taken in autumn, so no worries about residue.

Honey is one of the most natural products you can buy and because it has such a high concentration of sugars, it needs no additives to make it last. All you get in a jar is what the bees collected (and in my jars the odd leg or wing or bit of wax capping).

Almost everything I produce in my own garden is organic because I'm too mean to spend money on artificial fertiliser and pest control, other than my great big tube of slug death.

Franken-Plants

One of the latest plant breeding developments is to graft a flavoursome variety of a high-value crop, such as tomatoes, peppers or cucumbers, onto a vigorous rootstock. It's the science that's been used with fruit trees for centuries, but now available on a disposable scale.

This hybrid vigour means that you are virtually guaranteed bumper crops of top quality veg providing you don't plant them against a north-facing wall or forget to water them. In fact, they sound like the ideal cheat, the perfect way for a beginner to keep up with the veg-growing Jones's. In fact, you could never have gardened before and suddenly there you are, producing the kind of crops that Bob Flowerdew could hardly manage in his multiple poly tunnels. "Oh," you smile modestly, "it's just beginner's luck."

They're not cheap though, £10 buys you three pot ready plants. For that kind of money I'd expect a grow-bag thrown in, a bottle of Tomorite and someone to come and water them every Tuesday.

But I'm still tempted. I'd be interested to see what kind of impact the *terroir* had on their prodigious growing ability.

Mangetout

Talking of crops that look after themselves, I'm a big fan of the mangetout. Although I've gone on a bit about producing mini veg, there are some vegetables in my garden that even I can't restrain in size. Runner beans, courgettes, rocket, mangetout, rhubarb all seem to be immune to the effects of the grump *terroir*. No-one's going to be using the word bumper, any time soon, but they do border on the abundant from time to time.

Carrots, cabbages, leeks, sprouts, broccoli, peppers, tomatoes, salsify, potatoes, Jerusalem artichokes, asparagus, spinach, butternut squash and sweetcorn all come out in reduced size, reduced quantity or become inedible green lumps, host to "bug world".

But the mangetout is an absolute star. It will virtually plant itself, go to find supports to prop itself up, flowers with no fuss at all, produces a ton of pods and then delivers them in a bag to your back door.

Giving in to Rhubarb

Some veg is hard to grow, other veg is hard to *stop* growing. We inherited a patch of rhubarb from Old George and nobody in our household eats it apart from my mother-in-law, so I've been trying to kill it for years. Not in an overt, "drink this weedkiller and die" kind of way; more out of casual neglect. Which I'm good at.

One year I left an old water butt and some paving slabs slap bang on top of it and it still managed to find a way up round the sides. Another year I stored some railway sleepers on the rhubarb and it figured a way round them too. Typical, I thought, everything in my garden that I want to live immediately has a limited life expectancy, but the thing I actually want to kill shows no sign of pegging it at all. Irritated, I dug two of the more vigorous crowns up and put them in the recycling bin to be taken off by the council.

To be honest I half expected them to migrate back like that trio of animals in Disney's *Incredible Journey*. You can imagine the voiceover for the film trailer: "This summer, two rhubarb crowns find themselves at a plant waste centre miles from home. See the incredible story of their journey back to the rhubarb patch where they belong."

Then I created some raised beds from the sleepers that had previously been used in the conspiracy to squash them and buried them right underneath some mulch matting. It was child's play to them. For a stalk that likes being forced it was the simplest of tasks to scramble to the surface once they'd found a way past the buried matting in a Harry Houdini style. I've given in to them and they now have a third of a raised bed to themselves. I'm learning to love rhubarb. It's much simpler.

The same goes for Jerusalem artichokes. Once you plant them, you're never entirely free of them.

Living with Leaf Lady

During an average ho-hum day she was the mortal Diana Prince, but whenever danger stuck its ugly head above the parapet she became Wonder Woman and would venture far and wide to fight for the causes of right.

On the other hand there is my wife who, at the sight of a stray leaf scuttling across our pristine drive, is transformed into Leaf Lady, the scourge of every free-blowing leaf that alights there. Even though they both have alliterative monikers and both fight a foe, (if you can call a leaf a foe) the comparison isn't quite the same. Whereas Wonder Woman had contour-hugging stars-and-stripes knickers, Leaf Lady favours the baggy look, popular in gardens everywhere. She also needs counselling for OCD.

Zero Tolerance

Leaf Lady has zero tolerance. And it's not just about leaves, it's me snoring, the children interrupting *Strictly Come Dancing*, the internet going down, selfish parking…

It all started when we transformed the front of our house from a couple of shrubby overgrown beds to a smart, block-paved driveway. Out went the evergreens, the teetering old 1930s front wall with its cracked plaster fascia; in came a new perpendicular wall in front of an elegant curved planting area and pleasantly mottled paving blocks as far as the eye could see.

I stocked the curved bed with some gorgeous shrubs direct from the RHS Plant Centre at Wisley (the Harrods of garden centres as far as I'm concerned). There were lights set into the drive for an upmarket effect, everything looked so…so neat.

In fact the transformation was genuinely so great that visiting friends would drive straight past our house failing to recognise it.

At the same time we had installed our first proper patio, a carefully configured pattern of sandstone paving slabs matched with a series of beautiful slate planters. Mrs MacDonald was rather hoping that the fence would be renewed in this rush of investment, but this was a Leaf Lady-driven project and her interest (hence my motivation) stopped at the fence.

And So it Begins...

"I wouldn't mind if they were our leaves..." was the comment that first set off the alarm bells. I noticed my wife had started putting a dustpan and brush just inside the front door and occasionally I'd find her out the front on patrol for any stray leaf that blew onto the drive. Occasionally she'd show me some of the offending leaves she'd found out there. "Look at these leaves. Where have they come from?" was the soon-to-be-familiar maddened rhetorical question.

At first it was just the drive that she insisted on keeping free of leaves to a Howard Hughes degree. But it wasn't long before the patio also became the subject of her attention and a no-leaf loitering zone. If they were leaves from our sugar maple or the fruit trees she would remove them with a small tut, but if they were ash or oak from a neighbouring garden, then her eyes would narrow, like one of those silent movie close-ups. She would not be happy.

The Ultimate Solution

As most husbands will know, it's tricky to introduce the notion of your spouse's mental instability in a casual way into conversation. So I didn't. Dubbing her "Leaf Lady" helped a little bit. That first autumn with the new drive was a testing time. I had my wife curtain-twitching at the front and I had Mrs MacDonald curtain-twitching at the back.

By the second autumn I'd come up with a brainwave. I bought her a leaf blower. She didn't see the point of blowing leaves from one place to another – and quite frankly, neither do I – but you can get ones that will suck leaves into a bag.

Now she is as happy as a gorilla with a new tyre, carting her leaf sucker round the drive, patio and garden, banishing every last stray leaf. These clever devices also shred the leaves en route to the bag, so you have perfect composting material ready to go. There's only one small unresolved problem in that particular area...

Compost

Take a look in any garden supply catalogue and you will see more composting solutions than you can shake a stick at (which in itself sounds like a gardening-ism – from the phrase "more angry neighbours than you can shake a stick at"). You can have slatted timber compost bins, black plastic dalek-shaped bins, revolving bins, tumbling ball bins, ventilated plastic bins with weird flaps, and bins that look vaguely like bee hives. Your every conceivable composting need has been met by garden suppliers.

However...

My ability to produce compost efficiently is way up there with my ability to attract nesting birds. What happens when I put leaves or grass into a compost bin would surely interest scientists.

Nothing happens at all. No decomposition takes place whatsoever. It's like the moment plant matter goes in through the top everything becomes cryogenically frozen. If the Walt Disney organisation wanted to save refrigeration costs on keeping old Walt icy fresh they could easily bung him in one of my compost bins and nothing would happen. Even if we smothered him with compost accelerator he'd still be safe.

This lack of speed in the composting department has left me with a magnificent five compost bins worth of material. I've tried bunging in the aforementioned accelerator and my grass clippings laugh at it.

The Wheelie Bin Dance

To the rescue has come the council's brown bin service. Forget the provision of schools and local services, Leaf Lady thinks it's worth having a council for this reason alone. The broken, potholed tarmac road surface at the front of our house may resemble stretches of downtown Beirut, but as long as they collect the growing array of bins, she's happy.

Because while we're not great at producing large quantities of fruit and vegetables in the Grump garden, when it comes to garden waste, we rock! Thus the brown bin gets filled to overflowing three days into its fortnightly cycle.

When that happens I am obliged to climb onto/into it and do the wheelie bin dance. A dance that is somewhere between morris dancing and grape treading with a little bit of Zorba thrown in.

This can be perilous if the bin is not set up in a flat location. My greatest fear is not of being injured but having to explain to hard-pressed Casualty Department staff that I sustained my injuries while falling out of a wheelie bin...doing the wheelie bin dance.

Compost News

Bizarrely, I find I have got myself included on a Recycle Now mailing list. I get emails that start with:

"Dear composting friend,

With Christmas fast approaching and the shops full of presents, decorations and festive food, we've got some great composting tips and ideas to see you through the festive season."

That's an array of tips and ideas I won't be reading.

House Plantswoman Extraordinaire

Now if you thought I was a bad gardener, my ineptitude and lack of ability pails into insignificance when it comes to my wife's treatment of house plants. When unsuspecting house plants get dragged back to our house in the back of her car, they don't see the outline of a suburban house, they see the outline of the Bates Motel accompanied by that screeching violin sound effect.

The reason for this is her bizarre watering regime. She employs what is known as the desert/mangrove technique for watering. The first stage of this is to forget to water the new house plant for a couple of weeks so that the leaves begin to wilt and the compost dries up. This is known as the desert phase.

After that there is a sudden guilty rush to give it lots of water all the time…which rushes straight out of the bottom of the plant pot. This is known as the mangrove phase. Similar to a tidal mangrove swamp, the water comes in, and goes out again, comes in, and goes out again.

This is the pattern of treatment until the plant is thoroughly exhausted and gives up the ghost.

The R.I.P.-per

Once she has killed them or reduced their survival chances to a small percentage she places the pot near the conservatory door for me to dispose of, like Marie-Antoinette handing back a small puppy that no longer amuses her. It is then my job to administer the *coup de grace* and find a suitable last resting place for the plant. All I can say to them is that I am very very sorry and it was nothing personal.

My Father the Patriarch

Writing this book has been cathartic in many ways because it has brought back a family reminiscence that means I can attribute a lot of my fundamental ineptness to my father. My father was a useless gardener too, and I've only just remembered.

For a short time, while my mother was in hospital, he was left in charge of gardening duties. Up until that point his sole contribution was to mow the grass. But that was all right because it involved a mower and a mower had an engine, and he liked anything with an engine. And also he didn't have to bend over too much.

Faced with the prospect of having to do some actual weeding he turned to a mechanical solution and bought a Sheen X300 paraffin flame gun. This made gardening much more interesting and also turned it into a bit of a spectator sport for us kids. I don't remember what time of year he used it, but it was very comprehensive. It not only burnt the weeds, it destroyed all the plants he was weeding around. We never saw it again. I can only imagine the conversation he had with my mother when she came out of hospital to recuperate in her lovely garden. Or ex-garden.

Like Father Like Son

The only reason I know it was a Sheen X300 paraffin flame gun is that they're still on sale and I bought one myself in a desperate bid to get rid of some invasive bamboo. Reading the instruction leaflet, which can't have changed since my father bought one, was like looking at the sleeve notes for an early 1970s vinyl LP.

It included the advice, "Use only paraffin with this flamegun. Never use petrol or other spirits as these could be highly dangerous." I think in mine and my father's hands that was probably a moot point.

The 79-Year-Old Boy Scout

On the other hand my father-in-law is a dab hand in the garden. He's approaching 80 now and always has whatever you need in a variety of bumbags (or, as our American cousins might call them, fanny bags, which is quite apt because they do allow him to fanny around).

In many ways they're like his life support system and the only time he ever takes them off is to sleep, shower or have heart bypass surgery. They have a number of zipped pockets and there is always a gardening theme to one of them; which usually includes a razor blade, a plastic bag, ice cream lolly sticks ("for splinting broken stems"), plasticised garden wire, a magnifying glass, two pencils, three rubber bands and *The Observer Book of British Birds*.

If you have a senior relative like this and want to compare notes as to what they squirrel away, other pockets typically contain; bottle opener, fuse wire, nail scissors, suitcase padlock + key, small calculator, superglue, Vaseline, sewing kit, small torch, three biros red/black/blue, three rolls of tape, paper clips, parking coins, various keys, a car tyre dust cap and a St. Christopher, the patron saint of multi-zipped bumbags.

Once when we all went on holiday together, he was stopped by some security jobsworth at Gatwick airport who saw this teetering 79-year-old, on a cheap charter flight to Majorca and thought, "aye aye, we've got potential Al Qaeda material here".

The bumbag was turned out and they confiscated the superglue, a thermometer, a corkscrew, nail clippers, two rolls of tape and a set of jeweller's screwdrivers. The threat of Geoff rushing to the front of the plane and threatening the pilot with a set of jeweller's screwdrivers was averted. Though for those who know him, the prospect of Geoff rushing anywhere, at any time, is just as scary.

Tree totaller

If you offered me a small arboretum instead of a garden I'd take it. Now this might seem a strange sentiment given that my wife has OCD about leaves that fall in our garden, but she only gets twitchy about other people's leaves. I love trees and would happily have a garden of grass and trees.

This kind of attitude is bordering on the minimalistic Japanese approach. They like trees, gravel and rocks. There's none of your colourful bedding plants or hanging baskets to perk up the dull bamboo of the Shinto temple, oh no.

Actually I'd probably need to have some spring-flowering bulbs under some of the deciduous trees; a clump or two of snowdrops, some daffodils, tulips and narcissi. A few fritillaries would look great along with the bluebells amongst the birch trees.

And now you mention it, yes, what about a rambling rose up through one of the trees. A drift of poppies would look good, and how about…

Tree Fellers

Thankfully there is no such thing as the RSPCT, the Royal Society for the Prevention of Cruelty to Trees. I would be in deep trouble if there were. If somebody dropped me into the Forest of Fangorn in Middle-earth, I think J. R. Tolkien's tree-guarding creatures, the Ents, would get me for abusing their fellow trees.

In court, my number one crime would be for maltreating a walnut. I was given a young walnut tree in the early 1990s by my friend John, planted it, moved house, dug it up and took it with me. I replanted it in our current garden. A year later, I realised it was in the wrong place and moved it again.

Five years later it had started to relax and get used to its surroundings and put on some serious growth when I decided we needed a new shed at that end of the garden and guess which tree was fractionally in the way…?

So now the walnut is in its fourth location and still surviving. Likewise a Victoria plum which had a trunk diameter of about six inches that I managed to move and not kill. And yes it has produced plums since.

Here We Go Round...

Something that deserves to be given a much harder time is my mulberry tree. I planted it so long ago I can't remember if it's a black mulberry or a white mulberry. Certainly it hasn't bothered to produce any fruit to confirm which variety it is. Unlike the two trees mentioned above it has enjoyed the same sunny location for ten years yet it steadfastly refuses to produce any kind of fruit.

This kind of sulkiness is not tolerated in the Grump garden. If it's an astute mulberry it should have worked out that I am possessed of a chainsaw and a large axe and I might be tempted to change the rhyme to "here we chop down the mulberry bush on a cold and frosty morning".

Bedtime for Bonsai

Buying a bonsai tree is like getting a pet dog that will live to 100. They are just so much responsibility. Once you start, you're committed. That tiny little root system in the weeny little pot can soon dry out and get undernourished. True, you don't have to take them for a walk every day or stump up for the vet bills (though wouldn't it be great to ring up a tree surgeon and say, "I'd like you to come round and look at my twenty-year-old Chinese elm...oh, never mind I'll bring it to you."

If Mr Bean's nightmare was transporting a valuable oil painting that he mustn't damage, mine is that I'm put in charge of a bonsai nursery with racks of 100-year-old trees to look after. At which point the water board turn off the supply, the water butts run dry and an unseasonal hurricane approaches.

Front Garden Tree Syndrome

What is it about magnolias that make people want to plant them in small front gardens? For four or five years the small trees look great as they produce ever growing numbers of gorgeous creamy white flowers each spring and the small standard becomes a large standard.

Soon they start to obscure the front window and begin to obliterate every other plant in the front garden. When they have got that to themselves they continue upwards to the first floor and start to threaten the path and the neighbours' front gardens. Instead of pruning them, moving them or getting rid, house owners seem powerless to do anything. They just stand and watch, under the thrall of a tree that really shouldn't be in their front garden.

It can happen with other trees, but magnolias are the double-glazing salesmen of suburbia. You can't seem to get rid of them.

Top Ten Useless Things in the Garden

I have assembled a collection of sure-fire garden misses, things destined not to work in my garden. Now, were this category to be expanded to include things I have made useless in my garden – well, there's probably not enough pages left in the book…

Bird Boxes

I'd like to know what percentage occupancy figure the nation's bird boxes get. At three separate locations I've been serially shunned by birds and I'd like to find out if I'm abnormal. They say that "birds of a feather flock together" – well, not in my garden they don't. So is it just me or are there many bird box virgins around the country?

I'd feel a lot better about my serial inadequacies if I knew that on balance 90% of bird boxes never got an occupant. Presumably if I got the RSPB's answer to Kirstie and Phil involved they'd say the box was fine, it's all down to *Location, Location, Location*. I keep putting it in the wrong place.

The only time I've successfully hosted proper wildlife was a few years ago. One night I walked into our old garage and heard a tremendous snorting noise from under the workbench. The animal sounded as big as a dog, but when I got a torch and shone it underneath, it turned out to be a hedgehog and three babies in a nest the mother had made for herself out of hessian sacks I kept under there. Hedgehogs can make a huge amount of noise for their size! The mother must have heard me come in and sensed a threat and started snorting.

Typically I used to leave the garage door that led into the back garden open and one day she must have wandered in and thought, "this'll be a good place to give birth".

Having been disturbed she and the litter were gone three nights later. I subsequently built a lovely straw-filled wooden shelter, placed it in the garden border…which was shunned as usual.

Plastic Herons

They're not heron deterrents, they're heron attractors. It's obviously a plot by the koi breeders of the UK to increase their turnover. Inside every plastic heron sold there is a secret transmitter broadcasting to herons at a frequency undetectable to the human ear. The message is: "There are fish here! There are fish here!"

Teenagers

Teenagers may share a great many human characteristics but they are a species apart. They would like to be nocturnal, have little control over their limbs and avoid the sun, which is something that appears from time to time in a garden.

Because if they're out in the sun they can't be behind a computer screen updating their Facebook profile, or inventing acronyms like LOL, ROFL and LMAO*. Give them a job to do and they'll do it badly, half-heartedly or too quickly in a rush to go off and do something else that involves moving pixels around. Gardens have as much cool as bingo or support clothing.

For instance I would never trust a teenager to water the garden because my son's definition of "watering the garden" is anything up to two watering cans. Whereas the phlox alone needs its own can or it gets limp and pathetic – very much the teenager of the garden.

Equally, I'm very suspicious about teenagers who say they're interested in gardening. They're like the young people who want to be referees instead of playing football. Something's not right.

*If you don't know what these mean, trust me, it really doesn't matter.

Dribbling Rock Water Feature

This consists of a rock that has had a hole drilled through its centre, up which a tube has been passed allowing a constant dribble of water to flow out of the top to be re-circulated through a collecting tank at the bottom. It's a cruel indictment of our society that old people should be mocked in this way. This water feature is just a reminder to them of what's going to happen sooner or later when they get to the home.

In practice, the top of the rock will go green and the whole thing will take on the air of a badly maintained public toilet, but not quite so smelly.

Bulb Planters

This is the small garden spring-loaded tool designed to make planting bulbs easy. Ha!

Made out of the kind of flimsy steel that would find rice puddings a challenge, they are ill-equipped at burrowing to a depth of six inches into the lawn. You get about an inch below the turf line and despite face-contorting levels of pressure applied through the handle, that's as far down as they want to go. Apply further pressure, the metal bends and the mechanism jams up irreparably.

You're left with the choice of burying a lot of shallow bulbs or getting the spade out.

Trowel Sets

And talking about flimsy metal, there is nothing so annoying as a fork and trowel set. I am not a strong man, but I seem to possess superhuman strength when given one of these gift items. I can come straight out of the house having failed to take the top off a jar of mayonnaise and at the first contact with soil, the trowel handle will bend double under the less-than-mighty Grump forearm.

These trowels would probably be all right dealing with dry sand, compost, or TV soil, which as we all know is not real soil but a fluffy brown artificial substance. But when they come into contact with the real thing their tensile strength deserts them.

Anything Solar-Powered

God help the future of our planet if the range of solar-powered devices for the garden are an indication of where we've got to in converting the sun's rays into a valuable resource. I'm keeping my fingers crossed that the solar-powered lights and fountains we get offered use technology that's at least ten years out of date. Like most of the seeds that I plant, actually.

Maximum / Minimum Thermometers

You sometimes see them advertised as mercury-free thermometers, well mine are more like accuracy-free thermometers. I have two, placed side by side, and they're both wrong. One will say the temperature is two degrees centigrade while the other will say it's six degrees and I could probably have guessed that it's somewhere in between anyway.

I don't know about you but I love playing the amateur meteorologist. Being male of course I want to know about the extremes – the coldest days, the hottest days, the number of days without rain, the amount of rain. We get so much weather in the British Isles we should rejoice in it.

It can't be long till you turn up at the garden centre and find that they're selling your very own mini weather station complete with a wi-fi link to your home PC. This new bit of kit will give you all the current temperatures from a range of sensors in your garden – one in the greenhouse, one in the beds, one by the pond. You'll be able to plot temperature rise and fall across a week, a month, compare the data year on year, it's going to be an absolute stats fest.

If it's on the PC then you could probably access it remotely and so while you're on holiday worrying about if the garden's drying out, the mini weather station will be able to give you all the answers you need (instead of looking in British newspapers that are two days old to see what the UK weather forecast was).

Mine won't work properly, but I'm resigned to that.

Ultrasonic Mole Chaser

We have friends who have a holiday house in France who were plagued by moles on their lawn and bought one of these to get rid of them. Basically it's a big metal spike filled with batteries that you impale into the ground. Once installed it emits ultrasonic noises to deafen those noise- and vibration-sensitive moley creatures.

The trouble is, because the human ear can't hear it, you never know when it's stopped working. So you keep having to dig the thing up to test the batteries. One time they knew for certain that it had stopped working was when they arrived in Brittany to find a mole hill right next to the ultrasonic mole chaser. Then the time after that a friendly neighbour decided to cut their grass for them and decapitated the device. There was no discernible change in mole activity afterwards.

Presumably the same thing goes for ultrasonic cat and fox chasers that you see on sale in garden centres. You must have to keep checking those batteries too. I can't help feeling that a hungry fox will put up with a bit of earache if it senses food about, especially chicken tikka masala, which they adore.

Garden Plans

I'm a big fan of the improvised garden. I prefer the let's-change-the-garden-as-we-go-along approach. I don't understand people who see a big space and embark on a grand plan. That's gardening Marxism comrade! How do they know what's going to grow well in every aspect of their garden?

And why deny yourself the thrill of a chance buy at a garden centre by rigidly defining The Plan for your garden for the next five years. Obviously you have to plan where you put the paths and the hard structures. You don't just put in a drift of casual sheds on a whim, but my firm belief is that gardens should evolve.

It's also much less work.

Gardening and the Media

Most keen gardeners are also avid consumers of gardening media. Which is one thing we do very well in the UK. We may be slipping behind Belgium, Paraguay and Krygyzstan in terms of world influence, but our gardening programmes are second to none.

We've always had great communicators on radio and television, stretching back to the days of Percy Thrower on television and Clay Jones on radio. There's hardly a character I'll cross the room to switch off – Carol Klein, Chris Beardshaw, Rachel de Thame, Gay Search (surely a hobby in itself), Monty Don, Alan Titchmarsh are all fantastic TV presenters. Eric Robson, Pippa Greenwood and Bob Flowerdew are similarly brilliant to listen to on radio.

I have to confess the one that looks like Gollom from *Lord of the Rings*, Joe Swift, isn't a favourite, though. You keep on expecting him to gurgle "precious" in the middle of an item. Maybe it's the eyes.

Harder Than it Looks

What is slightly worrying for TV and radio gardeners is the attrition rate that goes with the job. We lost Geoff Hamilton at 60 and *Gardener's Question Time*'s John Cushnie at 66 with heart attacks, and Monty Don had a minor stroke at 52 which made him pass on the *Gardener's World* baton.

It's hard to sell gardening as a relaxing leisure pursuit when there are so many stress-related casualties at the top. I suppose I am so inured to miserable failure whenever I put on the half-serrated wellingtons, that anything which grows normally I see as a raging success.

Presumably at the top level of horticulture, (and I have to presume this because there's no way I'm going to get there) everything you do is under close scrutiny and has to be a success. Things have to flourish. And they have to grow to a timetable that shifts with the vagaries of the British weather. Which makes Alan Titchmarsh's robust and cheerful disposition even the more remarkable. So you won't have me knocking garden presenters. Apart from the one that chases the fat hobbits.

TV Soil

What you *will* have me knocking, though, is that unique substance – gardening TV soil. Where do they get it? I reckon there is a conspiracy at the heart of TV gardening related to TV soil. With the complete obliteration of any kind of ITV gardening output the BBC have cornered the market in soil close-ups. This means they can ship in their secret formula soil, the all-purpose, beautifully friable, rich soil that doesn't bear any kind of resemblance to the sticky, stony gloop I have in my garden. And no-one's going to challenge them because that's what we always see on screen. It's TV soil.

The BBC must have a central depot housing 200 tonnes of TV soil. The minute a new gardening programme gets the green light the call goes out. "Scramble the digger, we've got a gardening series in Tamworth, we'll need soil close-ups!" And then a crack team of BBC-trained operatives set out to exchange the unworkable "normal" soil in these gardens for their own tried and tested TV soil. Participants must sign some kind of confidentiality clause not to reveal that they have had delivery of TV soil and to deny its existence. I bet if you went up to the people involved in *Charlie's Gardening Neighbours*, where Charlie Dimmock got a whole row of neighbours together to complete a gardening project, they'd all completely deny it. Proof if ever you needed it.

Knobbly Edge in Wyre Piddle

As most of you know, the garden in *Gardener's World* has moved around over the years – from Shropshire to Worcestershire to Rutland to Hampshire to Herefordshire to Rutland to Warwickshire. From time to time presenters of *Gardener's World* try and throw in some kind of subterfuge, an embroidering of the TV soil conspiracy, alluding to particular characteristics of the soil in that part of the world. But it was all the same really.

That uniformity of soil is also evident in the mind-numbingly bland names the BBC have chosen for the gardens over the years – Barnsdale, Barleywood, Berryfields and Greenacre. Why can't the producers chose an unusual name and a striking location, such as Knobbly Edge Farm near Wyre Piddle in Worcestershire. Or try and find a garden in Badger's Mount, Kent, or Clay Bottom near Bristol or Crackpot in North Yorkshire.

You could imagine the humour that Alan Titchmarsh could have squeezed out of his parting shot at the end of the programme. "We'll see you next time at Crackpot, until then, enjoy your gardening."

A missed opportunity.

Barnsdale Equals Half a Pint

The producers probably never realised there was a student drinking game based on how many times Geoff Hamilton would mention the word Barnsdale during a broadcast. Every time Geoff would refer to "Barnsdale" you had to drink half a pint.

It's a tradition that was richly amplified by his successor and "Barleywood" but we'd left college by then. I think when we stopped, the record was four and a half pints, which is a lot for a half-hour programme.

That was back in the days when you had one TV in the halls of residence and the horticulture students insisted on watching *Gardener's World*, if only to prove how many latin names of plants they knew.

Gardener's Question Time

I don't make a point of listening to it, but if I switch on Radio 4 and it's on, I usually enjoy it. You see there's only one thing that puts me off *Gardener's Question Time* and that's the blinking gardeners!

Not the panel of experts, the creaking wavery-voiced old fogies they get on the programme to ask questions. The broadcast could be 15 minutes shorter if they just got a move on and asked their damned questions quicker. Instead we have to endure good old Cyril from the Daglingworth and Michinhampton Common Garden Society, tottering up to the microphone with his question in his trembling hand. "I… have… got… a… north… facing… wall… on…which … I… planted…" It's excruciating.

It's a much better programme when they answer letters from the studio. But like all programmes on Radio 4 if they dared to change the format there'd be a lynch mob of wrinklies converging on Broadcasting House in a fleet of Honda Civics hell-bent on ramming a sharpened Zimmer into the Director General's shins.

Though I'm just as bad. Whenever Eric Robson isn't on I'm not happy. Weatherman Peter Gibbs sounds a bit like "Keith the helpful accountant" doing his best to cover a gap when Eric's not there. Clay Jones and Eric Robson are very big shoes to fill.

Auricula Theatre

I'd love to have an auricula theatre just to wind people up that I was a theatre manager and I had my own little theatre in the garden. In terms of putting bums on seats it's not the greatest evening of entertainment you could wish for – two or three rows of primroses in a glorified cabinet, no curtain, no lights, no thrill of the greasepaint, no songs and very few dances.

When they're short of things to do in spring, television programmes often run features on them because there's very little else in flower at the time. Once every 20 years is fine by me.

During the *Gardener's World* Cultural Revolution, (a few years back) when they were trying to change the programme format round and bring in younger viewers, and viewing figures plummeted, you could imagine they would have had a much different take on auricula theatres.

Seeing as the BBC has become obsessed with finding stars

for the latest Andrew Lloyd Webber production i.e. *Sound of Music, Joseph, Oliver, Wizard of Oz* – they could have had a weekly programme featuring 25 auriculas hoping to make it through onto Toby Buckland's auricula stage. Viewers could vote to keep in their favourite auricula, whether it be edged, self, striped or fancy.

To make it more like the Saturday night programme, it wouldn't be the best auricula that got through – it would be the one with the tragic back story that was on a "journey".

Come Garden With Me

You should know the *Come Dine With Me* format by now, four strangers take it in turns to host a dinner party over four nights and get to bitch about each other's food. There's a lot of backstabbing and one-upmanship and it makes for great television.

How long is it before we have *Come Garden With Me* where four strangers are given four different allotments and are asked to produce a bumper crop of vegetables. Each invites the other three along to see what progress they are making and so we can have the bitchy back-of-the-taxi chats as they criticise what their fellow gardener has been doing. Except being a green gardening programme they should be asked to cycle home. The perfect person to host it would be the gorgeously bossy Helen Yemm. She'd whip them into shape.

In fact they could make it a two-part challenge. After growing the veg, competitors then have to cook a delicious meal with what they've harvested. A kind of *Come Garden With Me And Come Dine With Me Afterwards*. This is a series just waiting to happen.

The Gardening Apprentice

Or…have a programme entitled *The Gardening Apprentice*. It can't possibly be as bad as the one they have on BBC2 with the Earl Sugar. Or is it Viscount Sugar? You know I'm sure Alan Sugar's got some kind of title but it's so rarely mentioned I forget what it is.

We could have Lord Alan Titchmarsh in charge and it could be a kindly version where everyone is nice and tries to get on. They could be set tasks in parks departments, plant labs, at Nine Elms, in florists, garden centres, on farms, it would be a hoot.

Failures, Failures, Failures

A few years ago when they had all that rumpus about rigging the telephone votes on TV shows and fixing competition winners, the broadcasters set about putting their house in order. They weren't going to fake anything any more. No, no, what you saw on TV was exactly what happened.

I'm not sure that's entirely true when it comes to gardening programmes. I suspect that when the plants turn out to be miserable failures the item gets canned. I have a vague memory of a lake someone created on *Gardener's World* that steadfastly refused to be filled with water. That was obviously too big to substitute with "one they'd made earlier" and their failure had to be included in the programme. That's the kind of item I like. And it made me suspicious over what else had gone wrong which they could cover up more easily.

Because constantly thrusting success down other gardeners' throats is like being the size zero of gardening. It's a model we can't possibly emulate. We're only human, we like to see other people mess up, it makes us feel less like miserable dunces. We know the programmes are supposed to be the showcase of gardening, but, into each life a little rain should fall.

What we need is the Gok Wan (*How to Look Good Naked*) of gardening to make us comfortable with our size 16-18 abilities…oh, all right…and my 22.

Slug Balancing

There's a curious right-on-ism about gardening programmes that defies logic. On the one hand they're keen for us to look after the environment. On the other they organise gardening events at big showgrounds round the country getting people to drive a long way and expend all that carbon to get there. They can't have it both ways.

In the old days Geoff Hamilton was very into making stuff out of bits and pieces – probably because he had time. Alan eased us back into not feeling guilty about buying the occasional thing instead of making it or propagating it – probably because he was too busy writing best-sellers.

To my mind, you either have to adopt the purist, Bob Flowerdew, organic make-do-and-mend approach to gardening, or check your gardening self-righteousness at the door. You see half of me thinks that Bob is right, and the other half thinks I'd look stupid with a ponytail.

You might be kind to slugs, find organic solutions to all your pests, drive a modest car, recycle a lot and eat only locally grown veg, but if you've got a medium-sized pet dog you've still got a bigger carbon footprint than someone who drives a Toyota 4x4. The land and energy needed to produce pet food for an animal is shockingly large, the bigger they get, the more it adds up. There is some research that says a large dog is on average double the carbon footprint of that supposed totem of indulgence, the 4x4.

I don't have either a dog or a 4x4, I just have slug pellets, but it irritates me when gardening programmes suggest that doing some small thing a certain way should be verboten, making me feel guilty, when there are massive implications to many of the things we do that are never even discussed.

Those Pesky Meddling Scientists

How long will it be till we get a garden programme talking about planting a new crop of genetically altered sweet corn, or tomatoes? Or how about the new genetically modified melons that ripen in our climate and don't require thousands of air miles to get here?

As much as the garden media shuns GM seeds and crops with their, "Ar, it baint be natural" approach, it is the future and it will come whether we like it or not. Looking back in 50 years' time, our grandchildren will laugh at our fearful attitude to GM crops and our luddite opinions. We will appear like the peasant villagers in a Hammer House of Horror movie, lighting torches and threatening to burn down the houses of the kindly plant scientists who just want our crops to grow without disease and nobody to go hungry.

For years East Anglia's farmers could have been planting sugar beet that has an in-built resistance to fungal attack. It would mean less spraying of the crop with fungicides, less fuel consumed by tractors and greater soil quality for not being compacted by several passes of a heavy vehicle. But it's not allowed because it's that most evil of music hall villains, a GM crop.

The Clone Ranger...and Pronto

I'm not an evangelist for GM, I just don't see that it's particularly different to the manipulation we do to plants anyway. The reason we can all have an amazing new variety of clematis when it comes on the market is because of plant tissue culture – plant cloning in the laboratory. That baint be natural neither. Nobody asked the grapefruit if it was okay with being crossed with a tangerine to create the "Tangelo", we just went ahead and did it.

We breed vigorous rootstocks that start off in life hoping to be a fully-grown fruit tree, then CHOP! off with its head and on with a wimpy graft that has underperforming phloem and xylem. But that's okay, we're cool with frankenplants.

And nature isn't exactly an angel. Left to its own devices it's managed to give us a disease that has wiped almost all the glorious elms of our countryside and one that is threatening to do the same for horse chestnuts. Bees are disappearing thanks to the tracheal mite varroa. Thank you, Mother Nature.

Plant breeders are working hard to try and produce unmodified plants that ripen sooner, crop bigger, taste better and carry resistance to the natural plant diseases. It takes many many years to achieve that. They could do it so much more effectively if they were allowed to do a bit of genetic cheating.

Scientists may indeed have found an answer to the problem of the disappearing honey bee. They have discovered that if they can change a small part of the genetic code of the varroa mite they can probably stop them sucking the life out of bees. However that would be genetic meddling with an organism that was higher up the scale of living things than plants, so what to do?

Kill the blighters I say.

Jobs to Avoid in October

There are so many jobs in the summer that skiving off is rarely an option. But by October the football season is beginning to get interesting and it's time again to avoid the jobs that journals think you should be doing. Once October is over you can start pleading the cold and you are into a rich vein of excuses without having to get inventive.

Complete the trimming of your topiary.
That won't take long.

Pot up your spring bulbs at fortnightly intervals for a staggered spring display.
Or alternatively, plant them all together but put some in deeper and at right angles to give them more to think about.

Finish planting spring bulbs by the end of this month.
Now Old Horace used to swear that you could plant bulbs till the middle of January if you wanted to, but then again he did often have a lot of stock still hanging around after Christmas. This is certainly something that can be tided over till the middle of November or my name is not Ivor Grump.

Plant out biennials in the position they are to flower next year.
Yes, but at the same time have a word with the foxes and squirrels to make sure it's not where they intend to undertake exploratory work for the new trans-Surrey rail tunnel.

Check alpines for signs of rotting foliage.
If you can find them, that is. My first and last attempt at a rockery ended with my delicate collection of sedums and choice alpines being overrun by a rampant clump of geranium Johnson's blue. Which is kind of like the garden equivalent of letting someone sleep on your sofa for a couple of nights and then have them move in.

Move tender plants indoors ahead of any frosts.
This can easily be left till half-term at the end of October. We never get frosts before then. A little bit of cold's not going to hurt them over much and wrapping a plant in fleece looks a bit mummifying. That can probably wait till mid-November as well.

Worm casts become ideal weed seedbeds when trodden into the grass, so break them up or remove. What, and spoil all the blackbirds' fun?
They love knocking worm casts about in autumn. If you obsess about your grass as much as my brother-in-law or my neighbour, The Weasel, then you might be tempted to do this, but as far as I know it's only professional lawnsmen, such as greenkeepers, who bother. In fact this could be a new term we should use alongside "plantsman". You could have lawnsman for lawn specialists and treesman for a man of the trees. Not forgetting patio containersman.

Run the greenhouse heater and check that it is working before the frosts arrive.
Now I may be a garden numpty but I reckon a paraffin wick that worked last winter is still going to be working the following winter. Of course I could have inadvertently destroyed the gauze flame-guard with a misplaced size 11 in the spring, but the basic mechanism should work well enough. Whether I've got any paraffin or not is a far more searching question.

Lightly prune mophead and lacecap hydrangeas, cutting back to a healthy pair of buds.
The trouble is Leaf Lady doesn't know the meaning of the

words "lightly prune". She thinks if she doesn't attack a shrub and reduce it to a twiggy stump, it's got the better of her. Hydrangeas occasionally recover from one of her short back and sides prunings but for a lavender, her approaching footsteps mark the end of the line.

I Don't Want to go to Chelsea

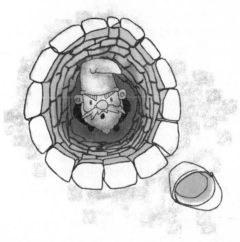

Elvis Costello and I have got something in common, though I doubt he was singing about the flower show in his 1978 single. I've been twice and once was probably enough. The overwhelming first impression is that it'd be quite good if they had double the space. In fact if they just made it a show for flowers they would have enough space. Instead they fill it with eye-wateringly priced gardening flotsam. It's not the best or most innovative ideas that get to Chelsea, it's the ones that are flash with the cash. Because space is at a premium, so the premiums for displaying your wares go through the roof.

Show Gardens

If you're an ambassador and need an expensive £250,000 garden to impress and entertain your prestigious international guests then Chelsea is a great place to come for inspiration – maybe you could even buy one off the peg. For you a £100,000 mirrored glass waterfall is not too much of a problem, neither is a set of bespoke hand-carved benches in Iona granite or for that matter a small avenue of 20-year-old pleached hornbeams.

Chelsea is full of impeccable set-piece gardens that look great to stroll through for five minutes but would be a nightmare to live with. I look at this annual parade of the impossible and imagine what it's going to be like in a year's time, stained by algae. They're gardens designed for lives nobody lives. Unless you're constantly whipping out the champagne, canapés and Ferrero Roché. How many are actually child friendly? "Remind me, Perdita dearest, what is a child?"

And the thing is, you can't even stroll through these altars to ostentation, you're limited to gaze at them from one end of the garden like a nosy neighbour. That's if you can jostle yourself into position for five minutes. I'd be quite keen to enhance the voyeuristic experience by putting a six-foot fence all along the avenue so passers by can't see into the show gardens merely by walking along. You would have to mount a raised walkway and peer over the fence, thus enhancing the whole snooping thrill.

The Nissan Sunny Garden

What's even worse than the sterile show garden, which is just a bit of planting round some fiendishly expensive hard landscaping, is the garden that recreates a "garden of old" or "a garden by the sea" or "Great Uncle Fred's allotment". What is the point of having a garden tableau unless your sole aim in life is to invite people round and say, "Guess what my garden reminds you of…?"

It's not exactly inventive either, you just get an old photo of an allotment, identify the plants and buy them. Done.

In a bid to be different and stand out, the show gardens are becoming distressingly like entries for the Turner Prize. How long is it until Tracey Emin or Damien Hirst get an entry? In coming years I fully expect to see the Car Wrecker's Garden, piles of wrecked and rusting Austin Allegros, Ford Escorts and Nissan Sunnys stacked on top of each other with a burst of asters planted at the bottom, a few intertwined buddleias and the occasional white or pink valerian poking through.

The Rain Garden

Diarmuid Gavin has produced some unusual and highly idiosyncratic gardens in the past and it's as a tribute to him I'd like to present my own idea for the Grumpy Garden at Chelsea.

The Grumpy Garden's theme would be – "it's always raining" – and my show garden would be dedicated to precipitation. The centrepiece would be a hundred coloured plaster hedgehogs in the shape of a rainbow. There would be a shelter made out of 20 slate umbrellas (a la *Umbrellas of Cherbourg*), a water feature that sends a spout of water onto a variety of surfaces – glass, acrylic panels, aluminium sheet (echoing a greenhouse, a carport and the caravan roof on a miserable wet holiday in Cornwall or Wales). Planting would be a generous assortment of moss, lush ferns and plants such as *crambe cordifolia* with billowy white flower panicles that look like clouds.

I'm sure the Meteorological Office would sponsor me.

Statuary at Chelsea

I love the odd statue and there are usually quite a few odd statues on sale at the show. You look at it, admire it, imagine the price, look at the price tag, and then have to add two zeroes to the price you first imagined.

Come the Glorious Revolution

Now I'm not saying that we should eliminate the £250,000 show garden entirely. In the glorious autocratic state that is the Grump Republic, it would still have its place.

Just as we have the Tate Modern to remind us what can happen if you give arts organisations too much money, so we should have some high horticultural art with a hefty price tag.

Incidentally, the whole bogus nature of modern art was illustrated back in 2010 by a "piece" at Tate Modern that had a gardening theme. Chinese artist Ai Weiwei filled one of the turbine halls with a hundred million porcelain sunflower seeds, inviting people to "look more closely at the Made in China phenomenon and the geo-politics of cultural and economic exchange today" by walking through the seeds. But when it became too dangerous because of all the dust they stirred up, the Tate had to ban people from going in there and walking on them...

So why wasn't it removed? If we have to respect the artist's integrity then we must experience his creation as intended, and it was intended to be walked round.

But I digress, my plan for Chelsea's show gardens would be to move the goalposts from year to year and force designers into some real invention. Right now we don't get the very best of British garden design, we get the best of those that can lay their hands on an enormous budget.

The Grump Agenda

Year 1: Show gardens would use only plants available in your average garden centre and limit the spend to £25,000.

Year 2: Something revolutionary – gardens with just plants in them. No angular polished steel conversation pieces, no hand-carved Etruscan sandstone terrazas, no bejewelled glass obelisks in shimmering emerald pools.

Year 3: Colour themes – choose red, white, blue or purple. It would be known as The Vita Sackville-West year.

Year 4: Gardens that evoke a national theme – for Holland; tulips, windmills and a clog-dancing animatronic mouse. It would be known as The Eurovision year.

Year 5: Gardens made from salvage with plants grown from seed. The Wombling year.

Year 6: Bankers' Bonus year. The kind of gardens that could only be created with a budget the size of a banker's bonus – i.e. like the ones now.

Bagging a Brugmansia

And finally Chelsea wouldn't be Chelsea without the scrum of the plant sale at the end. It's at times like this you realise that the event has been infiltrated by former members of the SAS in drag. "Little old ladies" are transformed into sharp-elbowed killing machines as they home in on that bargain buy and woe betide anyone who stands in their way.

Sundry Irritations

I like to think I have furnished you with a full inventory of garden grizzles and gripes, but on re-reading, there may be a few I've missed out. Fear not. As W. S. Gilbert once wrote, "I've got a little list". And the first of them could well come under the category of "society offenders who might well be underground and who never would be missed – they never would be missed."

Loud Women at Country Houses

Have you ever had this happen to you? You're visiting a country house on a beautiful summer's day, ambling along, admiring the borders of hardy perennials and marvelling at the handywork of the gardeners. All of a sudden you're assailed by this loud, pretentious voice – always a woman – showing off to her friend with a running commentary about which plants she can identify and which plants she grows. "I've got a simply wonderful rudbeckia just like that, attracts the bees like a magnet."

I know what I want to do, but I've never had the courage to do it. I want to go over and tap them gently on the elbow and say, "would you like a loud hailer?"

Plants I Will Never Buy

Plants you will never find in the Grump garden.

Silver-leaved artemisia. I don't know if it's a throwback to childhood but the thought of a silver-leafed plant in my garden makes me shiver.

Chrysanthemums, geraniums, marigolds and dahlias. One of the reasons that I know my wife – despite her obsession with stray leaves – is my true soulmate is that we hate the same plants. And we hate this quartet for the same reasons, too. They're rubbish. I think it might be something to do with their artificiality. They're like house plants that want to be taken seriously as garden plants. For some reason these are plants that the French adore. You'll see marigolds adorning French roundabouts and municipal garden beds throughout the summer wherever you go. Normally in rows, the French love planting things in rows. There must be something in the *Code Napoleon* that says if you have five or more plants, they must be in a row.

When it comes to planning next year's planting regime Monsieur Le Parks Superintendent has a fairly straightforward job. Last year he planted 100,000 orange marigolds, this year he planted 100,000 orange marigolds. Hmmm, what to do next year…?

Alyssum the "carpets of snow" rockery plant. Can't abide it. For some reason it reminds me of old ladies but I can't think why.

Zinnia (See dahlia)

Calendula (See marigold)

Cineraria (see artemisia)

DIY Centre Garden Departments

There is nothing sadder or more bland than the garden department of the major DIY superstores. They are the beige, dralon three-piece suite of garden supply. The staff know nothing about plants and seem to care even less. In spring they get stocked with 2000 trays of bedding plants, a quarter of which are dried and shrivelled within a fortnight.

If you have any self-respect as a gardener, you will turn

round and walk straight out of there – but do take advantage of their very good cut-price tools, a rake for £4? Bargain.

I Don't Care What the Weatherman Says, When the Weatherman Says It's Raining...

They are the villains of the piece. Weathermen are the traditional whipping boys of gardeners everywhere and they shouldn't be. They're just trying to do their job. What really annoys me are the people who blame weathermen when they don't get the precise weather they were predicting. It's not a blinking bus service!

The television forecast on the BBC is incredibly detailed and most of the times impressively accurate. If you watch Formula 1 motor racing you'll know that team bosses invest gazillions of pounds in predicting the precise time a rain shower is going to hit a circuit during a race, because it has profound implications on strategy. They even station helicopters in the air a few miles upwind to judge it. And they still get it wrong!

Although...

What DOES annoy me, though, is the person on the BBC website who puts up the single image to represent the weather for each of the next three days – Monday, white cloud; Tuesday, grey cloud; Wednesday, rain. I presume these are picked completely at random and then changed on a whim throughout the day. Even Paul, the famous World Cup predicting Octopus of 2010, could do a better job than they do.

You can look at it in the morning and the images are: Cloud, Sunny intervals, Full Sun. You go back mid-afternoon to check and all of a sudden the images are: Cloud, Drizzle, Rain. When you log in after work they have changed to: Plague, Pestilence, War.

Spits and Spots

The other thing that really annoys me is the "spits and spots of rain" phrase that they're always shoving into broadcasts, like they're trying to get it adopted into normal parlance. I've heard many people talking about rain over the years and we all know the phrases, "raining cats and dogs", "like stair rods", "chucking it down", "bucketing down" and worse.

I have never heard anyone say, "I'm going to take my coat because I think there might be a few spits and spots of rain later on."

It doesn't happen. Get over it.

Cold Snaps

The people who blame weathermen are the same malcontents that go on about Britain grinding to a halt whenever we get a cold snap. They moan that it's not like this in Sweden as they raise their eyes to the ceiling. No, it's not. Because they know it's definitely coming. And when they have winter it stays winter.

Sometimes we have bitterly cold winters. Sometimes we have winters that are milder than a dance critique from Torvill and Dean. My daughter was 10 before she had enough snow to build a snowman in our garden. When we do get snow, it's never for very long. All the time it's a transition between winter and spring and winter and spring, so it's far more difficult to adapt to than full-on winter for three months.

'I'm a Plantsman'

Just because you've got five books on perennials and know your way round the RHS canteen at Wisley it doesn't mean you're a "Plantsman". I'm getting a bit fed up of the self-aggrandisement of people describing themselves casually as a plantsman. Hyacinth Bucket ("pronounced bouquet") would no doubt call herself a plantsman, "it's gender neutral, darling," for snipping the odd dead head off her roses. She has the perfect first name after all.

Basically it's a major affectation to nominate yourself a plantsman. Other people can appreciate your knowledge and interest in plants and describe you thus but you don't describe yourself in those terms. For the same reason, I don't drop into conversation that I'm a painter, but I am. I don't exhibit much any more but if someone wants to come and see the two coats of blue that I put in the downstairs toilet they're very welcome.

I'll tell you the kind of people who are plantsmen; Roy Lancaster is a plantsman, Stefan Buczacki is a plantsman and

Keith and Ros Wiley who run the Wildside Garden Nursery in Devon are plantsmen.

Anybody who has ever planted more than one tulip upside down can never be given that moniker. I accept that.

Can You Be a House Plantsman?

I'd like to get into conversation with some self-confessed plantsmen and drop into the conversation that I, too, was a plantsman. When they talked about their rambling roses or their tiresome tradescantias I'd mention the difficulty I was having with my spider plant. The spider plant was at one end of the windowsill with a lily in the centre and a weeping fig I got for £2.99 from Ikea at the other. Quite a collection, really...

A Picture of Dorian Gnome

Have you ever been given a gift that you would like to take straight down to the tip, but are obliged to keep because it was a "carefully chosen present from a well-meaning relative"? My wife's grandmother once gave us a garden gnome because she knew we liked to spend time in the garden – not realising that the two are incompatible.

It wasn't the most unpleasant gnome in the world, more like one of those venerable rustic creations by Brian Froud, but it was still a gnome. When it was first unwrapped my wife swears that it was smiling.

The gnome would spend 363 days of the year in the shed and brought out on the two Sunday afternoons that the grandmother-in-law would pay a visit. Thankfully, after four years she died and we didn't have to carry on the pretence. Instead we started to give it to friends as a gift. If we went over to friends – who knew the story well by now – we would secrete the gnome about their house before we left.

When they paid us a return visit a few months later, it was their job to leave it somewhere obscure in our house or garden. We didn't refer to it, it was just done. After a couple of years the joke wore a bit thin and the arm got chipped, so I thought I'd put it out in the garden and use it as an air rifle target. It was then engulfed by the peonies for the summer.

When the Leaf Lady and I went about cutting plants back for autumn out popped the gnome. She took a serious look at it for the first time in many years and noticed it was frowning. As though constant maltreatment had changed its expression over the years from a happy smiling gnome to a miserable old git.

Whatever, it went to the tip.

The Wormery

They're a bit like the Breville's sandwich toaster of the garden – almost everyone's had one at one stage in their gardening career. I'd like to find out how many people who have bought a wormery actually got it to work. Up until the point I started writing this book I thought it was everybody except me. For those who don't know what it is, a wormery resembles the lovechild of a dustbin and a water butt, with a plastic lid clamped on the top and a tap at the bottom. You pile in kitchen waste and the worms set to it like it was a Pacman game, munching up old cabbage leaves, teabags and eggshells and converting it into beautiful compost with a rich source of liquid nutrient you can tap at the bottom. At least that's the theory.

I followed the instructions to the letter, created a home from home for my tiger worms – complete with a rotting vegetable feast for them to enjoy, closed the lid and left them to it. When I came back two days later with some sprout peelings, there was a couple of worms that had tried to get up and out through the lid, but I thought nothing of it. When I checked the wormery at the weekend there was no sign of worms at all.

I poked around a bit – nothing. They had all gone. It was only then that I realised the two I'd tossed back in were probably the last stragglers attempting to get out.

I went down to the fishing supply shop and bought some more – the same thing happened again. Due to my track record on all things gardening I immediately thought it was something to do with me. How rubbish was I? I couldn't even keep worms in a wormery.

Snap!

It was only when talking to a colleague that I realised I was not alone. "When we installed ours, it was like *The Great Escape* for worms," Katie sighed, "we put them in there and a couple of hours later they were legging it across the patio!"

Leaving aside the concept of worms "legging it" this was redemption. I'd always put it down to the fact that I was terminally awful at gardening but your basic worm doesn't like a wormery and prefers to take its chances with the blackbirds and the thrushes.

Or maybe the tiger worms you buy at tackle shops know they're going to be used as bait for fisherman and their innate instinct is to get away. They don't know that the thing you've dumped them in is a home from home. They might see it as an elaborate bait box and still feel the urge to flee. New to the market I've just caught sight of a deluxe three- and four-tier wormery. Presumably this is the Colditz of wormeries…

And Finally – You Know You're Getting Old When…

Be honest, when you were a child did you have a tremendous envy of competition-winning children whose prize was to run through a toyshop and grab anything they could stuff into their arms in two minutes flat?

That prize-grab lust changes as you grow older. When you're a teenager the toyshop becomes a record shop. When you're an adult it's a music equipment shop. And when you start on the downward path it's a garden centre. Congratulations, you're with me now. Though you better lengthen the two minutes to a sauntering half hour, and maybe throw in a trolley.

Grumpy Gardening Glossary

To help fellow gardeners understand and get to grips with the grumpy gardening lifestyle, I thought it only fair to provide a glossary of terms.

acid soil – Soil which is good for growing hydrangeas, rhododendrons, camellias, hibiscus and acers.

acre – A measure of land that requires you to buy a ride-on mower.

aerate – A scouse gardener finally admitting that you are correct.

air layering – Means of propagation which involves sticking a bag on the side of a tree and hoping for the best.

alkaline soil – Soil which is good for growing azaleas, hydrangeas, rhododendrons, camellias, hibiscus and acers with the addition of Miracid.

annuals – Garish plants that are usually best confined to hanging baskets and the French.

arboretum – The last place in the world you want to go round showing off your tree knowledge because they have the correct names underneath which will probably contradict what you're saying. And you can only get away with the excuse, "no, that *is* a kind of beech" once.

aquatic plants – Plants which will theoretically grow in water but don't count on it.

bare root – Normally the condition that hedging plants are delivered in. The Royal Mail will delay delivering them for weeks on end in spring, and then hide the package behind your gate where you don't find it for another two.

bedding plant – The kiss-me-quick hat of the plant world.

biennial – An annual that you suddenly realise hasn't flowered in its first year.

bolting – The action of small-minded vegetables that calculate exactly when you are going to harvest them and run to seed the week before.

bonsai – Plant mutilation as an art form.

botanical name – The scientific name of a plant, often with its discoverer's name tacked inelegantly on the end. They should never let people whose surname ends in the letter 'i' ever go searching for plants.

bud – A refreshing beer to enjoy in the garden.

bulb – Something you plant in the garden to keep the slugs healthy and well-fed all year round. Occasionally they will surprise you and emerge from the ground. That's the slugs not the bulbs.

cambium – This is the noise you make with your lips, seconds after swallowing a fly, in the process of establishing that it was indeed a fly you just swallowed.

catkin – The name of a girl who is going to be mercilessly bullied at school.

chlorophyll – The green pigment found in all leaves, stems and frogs.

compost – Organic matter that is nicely rotted and decomposed in a compost bin, after about a couple of weeks in most adverts and a couple of millennia in my garden.

conifer – Beloved by Leaf Lady.

crown – The part of the asparagus plant you shouldn't leave exposed to frost and if you do, don't be surprised if the whole blinking row fails to come up the following year, as if I didn't know.

cuttings – A sneaky method of reproducing the best shrubs that your neighbours have, particularly ones that border the pavement (but not limited to).

dead heading – Pinching off old blooms for tidiness sake. This process can be completely delegated if you live with a woman who likes her garden just so.

dibber – The police officer in *Top Cat*.

dethatch – De thing you put on top of de old cottage (sorry).

dividing – The process of splitting up perennial plants to show who's in charge and potentially to kill both of the resulting halves.

dormancy – The state you think that your divided perennial is in when really you have just killed a magnificent, thriving plant.

double digging – Twice the digging you expected.

double flower – A plant provided by mother nature whose single flower was clearly not good enough for know-it-all plant breeders who thought they could do much better. Normally a fuchsia.

drip line – Often found in the canteen of the local agricultural college.

epiphyte – Plants playing piggyback.

espalier – An expensive nursery process of training an apple tree so it grows in a flat plain. However the minute this tree is planted in the Grump garden, all its training goes out of the window and it acts as a normal tree again, with extra nobbles on to spite you.

evergreen – The colour attained by your gardening gloves.

fertiliser – Another name for a bag of Growmore. One of the greatest conspiracies in the world of horticulture is specialist fertiliser. Broadcasters, journalists and writers are all paid big backhanders by the agrochemical companies to recommend unnecessary feeds for this and that. All plants need is a bag of Growmore and they're lucky to get that.

flat – Technically this is a tray-like wooden box used to start cuttings, but also, with the addition of the word "perfectly", it describes the state of my lawn. Before I moved in.

foliar feeding – What caterpillars do.

forcing – This is the old, politically incorrect aggressive term for making rhubarb grow abnormally long. In this new PC world the phrase has been amended to "assisting the upward progress of".

frond – Leaf structure of a fern, or, a bloke you met after seven pints in the pub.

frost – The first indication that a grumpy gardener should bring his tender plants inside.

germinate – A rarely witnessed process where seeds begin the slow transformation into something vaguely like the picture on the packet.

girdling – The noise made by an elderly lady pensioner who has tripped and fallen into your pond.

grafting – When a grumpy gardener has been working continuously for 20 minutes without a cup of tea or a biscuit.

growing season – The part of the year which follows on

from the dying season. Not to be confused with the killing season which is all year.

hardening off – What happens in winter when you leave the greenhouse door open by mistake.

hardiness – The ability of a plant to withstand low temperatures when you leave the greenhouse door open.

herbaceous – Not a tree.

humus – Important element of a Greek *meze*, along with taramasalata and tzatziki.

hydroponics – Overwatering.

layering – What happens when you let a hairdresser loose with a pair of loppers and say, "Sergio, trim that tree…"

leaf mould – Theoretically something that happens in a compost bin.

loam – The word "loan" said after a visit to the dentist when the anaesthetic hasn't quite worn off.

manure – Something the local stable hawks round every spring as if you couldn't pick it up off the street for free.

microclimate – The very corners of my seed trays where in exceptional circumstances things may actually germinate.

micro nutrients – A good excuse for why your plants aren't thriving.

mulch – A layer of bark placed in the beds to suppress weeds and also to give something for the birds to do in the morning. They love tossing it onto the path to see if they can surprise the worms and grubs underneath. It's like the Nintendo Wii for blackbirds.

native plant – grass, dandelions and oak trees.

node – Something to watch out for when you're pruning. Apparently.

organic gardening – Another term for low-cost gardening. Organic gardeners are not allowed to buy anything or pass within 200 metres of a garden centre. Goods or services they wish to obtain, they must barter for.

organic material – Anything produced by an organism…or deposited by an organism, such as my neighbour, The Weasel.

parasitic plant – An epiphyte that has outstayed its welcome and begins to put down roots.

peat moss – Something that will have you ritually stoned if you go on television advocating that you like it.

perennial – A plant that lives in great fear of being divided if it grows too bushy.

perlite – Somewhere in Essex.

photosynthesis – A process not entirely understood by my wife who thinks that plants are happiest where they look best. Thus on a sideboard underneath a dark staircase is deemed a good place for a plant because it needed a bit of green and she is genuinely surprised when after a month it goes yellow and expires.

pinching back – Spontaneous pruning when you can't be bothered to go and get the pruners.

pistil – A great excuse to do the Mae West joke.

pollination – Sex for flowers.

propagation – Making more.

pruning – Trimming a vigorously growing tree or bush into a shape that broadly resembles the plant you started out with; only smaller, neater and not the horticultural equivalent of a toy poodle (see Topiary).

rhizome – The shout from a West-Midlander indicating that Ray is home.

root ball – Roots closest to the trunk of the tree that take on a familiar look after you replant it for the fourth time (see the Tree Totaller chapter).

rootbound – Roots that have stayed too long in the container and begin to emulate the M25 going round and round and round and not finding the right exit.

rooting hormone – Fairy dust that makes cuttings take hold despite your natural cackhandedness.

runner (doing a) – The art of finding something desperately urgent to do in the garden when your wife's friends drop by unexpectedly for a social visit.

scion – A new hybrid eco-car from Hyundai. Probably.

soil pH – The degree of acidity or alkalinity in your soil. Know it and you instantly achieve Garden Boffin status. Anyone who slips the pH of their soil into the conversation instantly receives the sarcastic moniker, "Professor" from me.

staking – Supporting a plant or tree with a stake driven into the ground. Technically you should put the stake in first when planting but my point of view is that they're lucky to have a stake in the first place, so get what you're given.

sucker – Someone who spends £100 in the garden centre the day before the sale. Beloved of Old Horace.

systemic – Pertaining to the plant's metabolic system. Adding the word systemic to a herbicide can add 25% to the price.

tap root – Always the last root to go when you're digging up a tree. Usually freed by rocking the tree from side to side while embracing it like the Boston Strangler.

tender plants – Plants which are unable to endure a Peter Gibbs weather forecast where the map of the British Isles is all in blue and he starts to shake his head sadly from side to side.

tendril – Cling-ons for climbers.

topiary – Pruning for show-offs.

topsoil – The very best soil.

transpiration – Perspiration for plants.

transplanting – The inevitable consequence of planting anything once.

TV soil – The soil used in any close-ups on a gardening programme. It is held in a large unmarked hangar somewhere in the midlands, and, like the recipe for Coca-Cola, its ingredients are top secret.

variegated – Plants with more than one colour and sometimes four – such as *Hydrangea quercifolia* quadra colour. Plants that have partly yellowed due to abuse don't count.

vermiculite – A great potting additive that retains moisture and air in the soil, made from the bones of crushed vermin, such as squirrels, foxes and mice. I wish.

Xylem – A musical instrument favoured by eccentric professors.